UNDER THE BRIDGE

Memories of a Garston childhood

John O'Neill

Copyright © John O'Neill 2011

John O'Neill asserts the moral right to be identified as the author of this work.

All rights reserved. No part of this publication may be reproduced, stored in a retrieval system, or transmitted, in any form or by any means, electronic, mechanical, photocopying, recording or otherwise, without the prior permission of the author.

Published by Arcadian Publishing

ISBN: 978-1-4466-4742-4

JOHN O'NEILL was born in Garston, where he spent the first 22 years of his life. He attended Holy Trinity Roman Catholic Junior School (1949 - 1956) before moving to De La Salle Grammar School, and thereafter to Liverpool University, where he graduated from the School of Hispanic Studies in 1966. Thirty-nine years blissfully teaching Spanish came to a happy end in 2005 with a move to Spain's rural north west, where he lives with Margaret, his children, and his beloved grandchildren. He is the author of "Of Castles and Caballeros: Travels in lesser known Spain" (May, 2010).

For Jo

fondest memories

of you and Erika.

John

Tourén, MARCH 2011.

To all the wonderful people herein mentioned; to Our Dennis and his extraordinary memory; and, most especially, to Catherine, who singlehandedly put it all together – my deepest thanks for your involvement.

For my Mother and Father,
Margaret,
Angela and Cael and Mia, angels all,
and their Parents.

CONTENTS

1. Uncle George and the wheelbarrow
2. John and Mary, Mary and John
3. There's only one Miss Murray
4. Ructions
5. Dream on, dream on, Teenage Queen
6. Ivanhoe at Christmas
7. Mr. Moore and things on the floor
8. Pigeons
9. Sammy and the stuff of minor legends
10. Stanley Whelan's bells
11. I remember the day …
12. Hindsight

1. Uncle George and the wheelbarrow

If you've got ten minutes or so, come and take a leisurely walk with me down Window Lane, meet some people I used to know, and listen to some anecdotes.

I say "down" Window Lane because from time immemorial that means starting at the Banks Road end, until you eventually reach as far as you can go, where you'll finally get to Blackburn Street (which isn't really a street at all in the conventional meaning of the word). From top to bottom, it's as straight as a die, and it's absolutely teeming with life in all its wondrous riches.

Now, on your right there, and barely noticeable since there hardly seems to be any commercial activity going on, is Corffe's. This particular Corffe – Jack's brother and a trader (a butcher, in fact) further down The Lane on the same side – apparently sells cigarettes and tobacco, fireworks, Christmas and birthday cards, toys you never see people buy, and runs a battery changing service for wirelesses.

And that – aside from the bus stop for the 66, just before it turns left into Banks Road on its way to Woolton and Belle Vale, Gateacre – is just about all there is until you get to Raglan Street. That's where you'll find one of the two Co-Op grocers, and just around the back is the Co-Op's own milk distribution depot.

Across the road, you'll see Larson's Ladies' Fashions. Thelma lives there with her parents: she's a remarkably pretty girl in an orthodox sort of way – clean and clear features, short black hair in the shape of a helmet, bright smile – and I'm not embarrassed to say that she was very attracted to me at one time far away and long ago. However, I am hugely embarrassed to confess that at the age of twelve I inexplicably rejected her out of hand. Shame on me! Eileen told me I'd missed the boat there.

Just beyond Larsons' and The Hillside Laundry and Bella Blackwell's Sweet Shop is Mrs. Parker's, The Newsagent. In spite of the fact that there was indeed a Mr. Parker very much in evidence, it was always known exclusively as "Mrs. Parker's". A very small, knotty woman, with a broad Lancashire accent, she spent most of the day behind the counter of the bus-stop-size shop that smelt (relatively) pleasantly of roll-your-own tobacco.

She sold newspapers and fountain pens and ink and what we'd now call 'girlie' magazines. Looking back over half a century you realise there was little about them that was even remotely sexually stimulating by modern standards. Eileen used to get the Reveille for Frank every week without fail, and she still ended up with only one child (not that she wanted more, mind you, and Frank's interest in further procreation was distinctly nil. It would be fair to say that the prospect never crossed his mind).

When sunlight was on her window, she'd send Mr. Parker out to extend a tarpaulin to protect the magazines on display. During my ostentatiously rebellious periods – one of many, I'm embarrassed to say, a poor man's rebel without a cause – she'd get me The Soviet Weekly, and I'd bask in the minimal, misplaced notoriety. Our Dennis used to think – until recently told otherwise – that I was an ardent devotee of Communism.

On dark, wet nights, we'd hear Mrs. Parker's heals tap-tapping down our back entry and beyond, going to see her sister, I think, somewhere at the bottom of Shakespeare or Otway Street. Going to see somebody, anyway. She wasn't a smiler, Mrs. Parker.

On the same side of The Lane – not many of the natives bothered with its full title: everybody knew exactly what you meant – and opposite the tiny Post Office, was Jimmy Lunt's. Depending on the day and the time and who you were and if you were a regular customer or not, he could be an awkward old bugger. Clad in an 'Open All Hours' brown apron-cum-coat, a fountain pen staining his breast pocket, chewing the same piece of bacon from opening to closing times, he'd arrive on his battered Raleigh (with its chain-guard) not long after seven in the morning.

Hams hung on either side of the narrow entrance passage, and shelves bulged with every tinned food you could possibly ask for, so much so that no more than three or four customers could crush into the shop at the same time. He'd close up around six, and be back an hour or so later, just to see how things were going. On his battered Raleigh (with its chain-guard).

Next door, in what was nothing more than the front room of an ordinary two-up-two-down, with stairs just inside the front door, was Ted

Fulton's. Ted cut men's hair in a fashion that never moved beyond the styles of The Great War. It always mystified me – more irritating hair down the back of my shirt than on the floor – when he'd lower his voice and ask adults if they'd like "anything for the weekend". Oh, innocence of childhood.

Gordon Wass and family – John got to the heady heights of lecturing at university, no less, and with an excellent reputation, to boot – lived in Shakespeare Street. So did Booie Hughes and his wife, daughter Sylvia, a recognised beauty by any standards, and Our Poor Malcolm (who aspired to little, achieved less, and sadly died young, in circumstances I'd rather circumvent, if it's all the same to you).

Where were we? Ah, yes, Shakespeare Street, named for The Bard, though that was hardly a consideration amongst the locals. On one corner stands Edward Arden's Clothes (and behind it, somewhere in the rear and – quite naturally – not drawing attention to itself, is the Pawnshop). Then, there's Waterworth's, the fruit and vegetable shop, and Woodsons (where Tommy used to work).

Being something of a young entrepreneur – or, more likely, needing the money for something now very long forgotten: an Ian Allen Train Spotters Book or a Charlie Buchan Football Monthly – I suggested to Eileen that I'd do the messages for her every Saturday morning for six pence. When it shortly dawned on her that this was indeed in danger of becoming a weekly event, that six pence was not something she could recklessly dispense with, I was met with excuses I couldn't fathom and redundancy at an early age. It shouldn't have surprised me too much, though. She'd often ask my Mother for "a lend of two bob, Liz" because she was loathe to change a ten shilling note.

We lived in Otway Street, the top end, in the first block, across from Georgie Darnell's and Old Mrs. Hayes (and Gerry, her quixotic son, who led, shall we say, a very inventive and invented existence), and Puddin English. Corrie's were next door to us; then Florrie and Norman and Sylvia, all in the one house; Eileen and Frank; and the Phillips' family, the daughters famed for being "nervous".

If you went out via our back doors you'd soon come to the back of Jack Corffe's, a perpetually genial man, and then Esther's. Go through her back yard, dodging the chickens and Old Granddad Darlington, flat-capped, fingerless gloves, dribble – and rimless spectacles on a string – on the end of his nose in all weathers, and you'll see Esther with Violet, a big, awkward girl, serving customers in her haberdashery. Look that word up in an old dictionary: it's not something you'll hear much used in this day and age.

Why "through her back yard?" I hear you say. Well, Esther didn't seem to mind if regular customers came in that way or through the more conventional entrance in The Lane, the bell tinkling when you opened it.

And if you look across the road from her front door you'll smell the super aromas from Humes The Baker, with everything from meat pies to coffee buns and everything in between, and the place is never empty (and positively heaving around midday, men coming up from The Bottle Works, and girls and young women from The Matchworks).

Just as full, though smelling differently, is Becca's Chip Shop. A natural red-head, pleasantly loud enough to be heard at either end of The Lane, Becca has an equally red-headed son, slightly fleshy and slow moving but good looking in a dissolute sort of way, and an ever-smiling husband, who seems to work outside of the one-woman family business.

And that was where I was around five o'clock on the late afternoon of 6th. February, 1958. Like everybody else, I was queuing around the side wall, then the back wall, and eventually to the head-high counter itself. Becca was keeping up a varied series of conversations with her customers, moving effortlessly from one theme to another, chip fat sizzling loudly: the 66 bus went by, it was raining indifferently outside, and I was asking for "six a chips an' three a peas an' don't forget the vinegar, please". That's when someone rushed in and told us all that a plane had crashed in Munich, killing a couple of dozen people, mostly young men in their early twenties.

Ainsworth's, next door, never seemed to close, Old Mrs. Ainsworth, glum Cyril's ancient mother, an ever present (though you'd never see her at first when you went in until she stood up from her stool to serve you, and even then you only got the top of her white head).

Then Davidson's, for bread and milk and associated items, where my Mother worked some mornings without my Father knowing; Atkins' Sweets Shop (later, a hairdressers); and opposite that the half dozen houses where the 66 bus made its first stop outside Joey Cooke's house after leaving its terminus at the bottom of The Lane, bound, ultimately, for Gateacre.

Though there were shops and landmarks beyond that – Durkin's Coal Yard, The Bank (an open space of rough, pitted land at the opening to Lincoln Street), Ted Fenlon's, Larson's Newsagents, The 99 Ice Cream Parlour, Doctor Franklin's Surgery, Houghton & Lappins, The Woodcutters, The Cant and The Clarence – these places were largely unknown to me until I was sixteen when I went to work as a temporary wages clerk during the summer of 1961, just after finishing my O Levels (Remember them? Proper exams!) at De La Salle Grammar School, Carr Lane East, two bus journeys away: the 80c to Penny Lane, then the twenty past eight 99 almost to its terminus. I loved it.

The Bottle Works was at the very bottom of The Lane, on Blackburn Street, which was basically nothing more than one long, open space on the front of The Bottle Works, extending on one side to the docks, on the other towards The Cast Iron Shore. It was little more than a five minute walk from Otway Street, and I got the summer job thanks to Bill Sephton, an enormously likeable man, whose back door looked across at ours from a distance of four feet.

Bill was single by choice, immaculately dressed, in an old fashioned sort of way, barbered and shaved to perfection. In the office, he religiously took his newspaper with him to the toilet for his working coffee break every morning and afternoon. He shared a desk with Bob Roberts, an amiable man who, aside from his work, spent the day trying to rein in his rebellious false teeth, lisping slightly when he spoke, blowing loudly to clear his nose and nasal passages, hands like shovels, ever ready to talk about "my two lads", clearly a case of mutual worship.

Margaret – fairly frequently absent from work and what you might call 'careful' about her health: I don't think she ever liked me, for some reason – always worked at the desk next to John, both of them, heads companionably close, quietly humming Gilbert and Sullivan tunes ("How about this one, then, Margaret? D'you remember this one? Oh, you must do!"), self-proclaimed experts on Anne Zeigler and Webster Booth. (Anne Zeigler – or Irene Frances Eastwood – was actually born in Liverpool. So was Jack Jones, by the way, and in York Street, not a stone's throw from The Bottle works. He was wounded in Spain in 1938 at The Battle of The Ebro. Now there's a thing! A local hero.)

Then there was Fred, in charge of the office by dint of seniority, and for whom everything was an hourly crisis. He was daily fond of "You go, I'll stay" when final totals were needed on Thursdays, traditionally pay-day; "It never rains but it pours"; "There's no future in history"; "Roll on, death"; "No rest for the wicked", and other such utterances of boundless optimism.

He'd come into the office like a whirlwind, dressed like a cross between a space-man and a yeti in his motorcycle outfit, and divest in front of everyone, giving a minute by minute account of yet another horrendous journey to work, all the way from nearby Aigburth, barely two miles away.

For the rest of the day – he religiously took no coffee breaks: "There's no time for such frivolities. This is a matter of life and death, a race against time" – he'd stand bowed over his desk, spectacles balanced precariously on the tip of his nose, sleeves rolled high, tight braces accentuating his round shoulders, saying "Dear-dear-dear-dear-me", or "I could just go some biccies and a nice cup of tea", never drinking the tea until it was cold and milk-rimmed, slurping noisily, biscuit crumbs everywhere, cackling to himself.

He couldn't abide blue jowled Malcom from Personnel, a cheerful, late twenty-something, an eternal optimist, whatever the situation. Fred didn't do optimism. It just wasn't right. Life wasn't meant to be enjoyed. But his attitude to both accountants was sycophantic in the extreme.

To Mr. Griffiths, a tall, enormously elegant man of meticulous dress and manners, Fred would drool his answers, bending low with a saccharine smile, chortling and emotionally out of control. But "That Hargreaves", as Fred called him when he wasn't bowing and scraping in his presence, was a man who favoured woollen suits with a loud check and clashing ties, heavy, expensive brown leather shoes which would announce his coming, an unpleasant Mancunian with an unpleasant Mancunian accent, and a vulgar line in language which made Methodist Fred visibly wince.

And then there was my Uncle George.

You should know from the very outset that Uncle George was in no way averse to hard work. He'd worked on Garston Docks, off and on, for years, and in economically difficult times he felt the need to help out his family with certain items – bananas, the famously lured Christmas turkey from down the entry with Sammy, the poor unsuspecting bird's neck wrung before it knew what was happening – which, shall we say, presented themselves to him as though manna from Heaven.

But George simply didn't see the point in unnecessary work when there was an alternative. So, when he got a job in The Bottle Works as a general labourer, he sensibly decided that whilst he'd do his best, he would look for simpler alternatives. He soon discovered that a company which then employed a considerable number of men in its various sections of bottle production could never hope to keep tabs on everyone in its employ. After much thought, he hit on an idea of startling, effective simplicity.

There were lorries and vans and fork-lift trucks all over the sprawling site, but George couldn't drive. Instead, he commandeered a decrepit wheel barrow seemingly no longer in use, walked it to the gate, with a few broken pallets on board, and convinced the man on the gate that he was delivering his load elsewhere, somewhere up The Lane.

Hours later, he'd return with the wheel barrow suitably empty, reporting his successful delivery. Not wishing to be over confident, he limited his forays to two or three times a week, anxious to avoid suspicions. How long this went on and what happened in the end I can't honestly recall. You might want to ask Our Dennis, if you really want to know, though I'm not sure he knows the true outcome, either. Perhaps the best alternative might be to leave things as they are, and ponder what is known for certain: sort of 'let sleeping dogs lie'.

In all likelihood, Uncle George tired of this adventure and discovered something new. He'd never have said it of himself, but he was what some people might have called mercurial, perhaps, or unconventional, or just plain rakish.

But he was never mean-spirited. No, never that.

2. John and Mary, Mary and John

We lived at sixty-three, Otway Street, Garston, Liverpool, 19, Under The Bridge. For many years – and this is true – I didn't realise that there was another Garston on the other side of The Bridge, extending beyond the Sir Alfred Jones Memorial Hospital and just before it became Allerton; beyond Saint Mary's Road, where it became Aigburth and leafy Grassendale; along Speke Road, near the railway lines and the stock yards.

And beyond all that, of course, in a sort of no man's land, was the social aberration that was Speke, a new estate where the Liverpool City Council powers-that-were, in their total lack of minimal wisdom and with an absence of sensibility that beggars belief, had removed city people totally unused to wide open, featureless spaces: no shops or facilities to speak of, apart from the 80 and 82 buses. A barely habitable waste land: and then they wondered why the experiment failed, over more than fifty years, to live up to their misplaced expectations. Of course, the legislators continued to live in Childwall and Crosby and other leafy glades.

Next door to us, at sixty-six, were Auntie Mary and Uncle John, no relatives at all despite the titles conferred on them. In those days, in Garston, many families had surrogate relatives who claimed no blood kinship with you or your family, but who lived with you and in your lives to a greater or lesser extent every day. Who shared your joys and your woes, who knew your personal business but seldom abused the knowledge, even in their daily gossip.

Take the Wilks, for example, painfully stuttering Hilda, and Jim, who habitually spoke like Donald Duck.

It wasn't uncommon for Our Alan (the oldest son, and someone who was very clearly deranged at the best of times, not at all of this world, where he didn't abide too long) to launch himself at Our Eric, his infinitely more intelligent brother, Hilda's bread knife in hand and baying manically for blood ("I'll kill him! I'll kill him!").

They'd start by kicking shit out of each other in the back bedroom for no reason anyone could subsequently explain. The scuffle would spill out onto the small landing at the top of the stairs, where Eric's more considered blows had rendered a spluttering, gibberish Alan speechless with rage and impotence.

He continued to wield the knife, now symbolically rather than with any hope of assassinating his brother, muttering unintelligible imprecations, until Hilda eventually and painfully overcame her stammer long enough to explain the pressing problem to Frankie Jones, across the street in number sixty-nine.

Frank, who was immersed in an article about Sugar Ray Robinson and Carmen Basilio at the time, and was less than happy with the interruption, put down The Ring, crossed the street, went up the stairs to the landing at the top, slapped Alan twice across the face, very hard, took the bread knife and gave it to a thankful Hilda, and went back to finish the article about Sugar Ray and Carmen Basilio, slightly miffed that he'd temporarily lost his place and train of thought.

Next door to John and Mary were Les and Doris and their two well mannered lads, Leslie and Steven, all living in the same house as Miss Kelly, octogenarian (and the rest), all toothless, slack features that always managed a smile and a word. Then came the Dixons.

Doris Dixon absolutely loathed Our Dennis with a passion, because, among other things, he back-chatted her on a regular basis and wouldn't "go and play by your own door". In fact, he took no notice of her and that, more than anything, infuriated her; until, having told him one too many times, by his reckoning, he retorted – aged ten, you might want to bear in mind – that she could "go and kiss my hairy arse".

Some time later, when she'd recovered something approaching her poise, and in spite of getting no support from her husband who rightly chose not to confront Our Dennis, she went and complained to Peggy. In accordance with long established ritual, Peggy did the needful and thrashed Dennis round their back yard and back, but with a marked lack of conviction since she was by no means a fan of Doris Dixon, whose come-uppance was long overdue, in Peggy's books.

Across from Dixons was the ancient Mrs. Hayes – there didn't ever seem to be a Mr. Hayes: perhaps he chose to remain in Sligo – massively older than she should have been with a son and daughter both in their early twenties. The son – 'boy' would perhaps be a more accurate description, given his questionable behaviour – was fond of telling epic stories without the slightest foundation, shall we say, with himself firmly in the role of the super-hero. The daughter, high heels, fishnet stockings, something that passed for a mini skirt long before they became fashionable, painted face, went wrong: let's charitably leave it at that. Mrs. Hayes always seemed to be crying, or perhaps it was her normal way of speech.

And next door to them, the Darnells, the mother a tiny woman with a constant look of bemused surprise on her face, ready to break out into a hysterical laugh where most people struggled to see anything approaching humour. And Georgie, all tight red curls, and spectacles that threatened at any minute to slide off the end of his nose completely, one sock up, one sock down, exploding from the open front door and up Otway Street to Window Lane on a message, breaking into a skip every few paces in his headlong dash. In spite of all his speed, Georgie was naturally friendly and well mannered and a credit to his mother and always stopped long enough to say hello to everybody.

Florrie lived at number sixty-seven with Norman (her elegantly dressed, beautifully barbered, middle-age son) and Sylvia, his childless wife, who never had less than a good word for everyone. By no means was it their fault that Florrie was out in The Lane at all times of day and night, in all weathers, talking to anyone who happened to pass by, whether they were willing listeners or otherwise.

"Did you hear what happened to her in Lucania Street? Awful! Awful, it was!"

She positively thrived on bad news and misfortunes of every size and shape, never happier than when she was the bearer of the news of a death or an accident or an illness or a divorce or some event or other. She was the first one, in later years, to report that Alan Wilks had been murdered, and she had a field day (even if they never did found out who did the dastardly deed).

She was the joyful recipient and bearer of any sort of bad news, and on winter's nights, in howling, horizontal rain, she'd stand on the corner of Otway Street in the hope of imparting bad news to anyone willing to listen, by which time her version had become many times more gruesome and colourful that the original event. "Isn't it shame? A crying shame, it is", she'd say rhetorically, and wait for a reaction. Though she did it all without the slightest malice, she was known all the way up and down Window Lane and the streets off it, and even, some said, up The Village as far as The Lyceum.

Between Florrie's and our house were the Corries. Mr. Corrie was, shall we say, somewhat 'mysterious' where work was concerned. Dressed impeccably in a navy blue sports coat, gleaming white shirt, regimental tie of questionable provenance, and light grey trousers, a thin moustache always clipped to perfection, he worked as a driving instructor of sorts, a bus conductor from time to time, and, he said, an important insurance man, though not all at the same time, for no great length of time, and for what seemed interchangeable periods of time. Unlike all his neighbours without exception, his speech was meticulous and clipped, but never unfriendly or class conscious.

His wife had the pudgy pallor of a woman whose health was never quite what it should be, though she, and her doctors, could never manage to define exactly the nature of her putative illnesses, for there were many. Like her husband, she spoke in a gentle, refined tone, and was never anything other than a model neighbour. On the countless occasions when one of our balls went over the wall and into their yard, it would be promptly returned without a complaint. Melvin, the older of the two children, severely short sighted in one eye and probably blind in the other, was fanatical about football, the original headless chicken, enthusiastically cannoning off everyone and everything in his path, including the back entry walls. Robin didn't like football.

My Auntie Eileen and Uncle Frankie Jones lived just beyond them. Frank never had a bad word to say about anyone. Eileen found it genuinely difficult to find a good word to say about anyone, though she sometimes tried. In spite of this, they did manage to get on for twenty years or so of marriage before tragedy struck them both in different, though related, ways.

Mr. Jump used to come to Eileen's, year in year out, on his old Raleigh, every Tuesday about one thirty in the afternoon. He was below medium height, bald headed except for a fringe linking both ears, wore a trilby and a light-brown, belted gabardine in all weathers, bicycle clips he was never seen without (even when sitting), and was The Insurance Man.

I've no idea how it all started – and you shouldn't read anything 'suspicious' into it. Eileen wasn't by nature romantically inclined: ask Frank – but Mr. Jump always had a boiled egg and toast-soldiers, fairy cake and a pot of tea in Eileen's. He was a jolly man, though softly spoken, with a kindly voice. My Mother would sometimes bring him a coffee bun from Humes' in Window Lane. If Peggy was around, she'd make her way up from her house on the end of the block. They'd all talk companionably about this and that, nothing very serious or contentious, and around mid afternoon he'd be gone, promising to be back the following Tuesday.

Then, all of a sudden and without explanation, Eileen answered his knock on the front door, briefly did whatever insurance business was to be done there and then on the front step, and Mr. Jump never again saw the inside of number sixty-nine, Otway Street. If my Mother ever knew the reason – and I don't think she did: Eileen could be secretive when she wanted – she never spoke about it. All very funny in a not very funny way, if you see what I mean.

There were three blocks of fourteen terraced houses on either side of the entire length of Otway Street, Garston, Liverpool, 19.

Strangely enough, and with very few exceptions, you limited your acquaintances to the people in your block of fourteen, and the block across the street, barely a dozen paces away. But Old Gilbert Ireland, who lived beyond our block, came up the street and passed our doors every day of his very long, very cantankerous life. Flat hat, untrimmed cigarette stained moustache, an ancient dark suit of unspecified colour, an off-white scarf wrapped around his neck and tucked into his waistcoat, hobnailed boots and a walking stick.

He really was a vicious old bugger. At any time of day, and most particularly during school holidays, kids would sit or play on their front steps, or on the narrow pavement in front of their own door. When Gilbert came up the street he'd walk slowly in a straight line and twat the legs or feet of any child too slow to get out of the way, curse unintelligibly, spit into the gutter, and be on his way to the top of the street and down The Lane.

Nevertheless, he was an exception (Doris Dixon and Our Dennis notwithstanding). People then, by and large, with all their foibles and failings, were generally nice to each other to a greater or lesser extent. And that's where – belatedly, you'll say! – John and Mary come into this account.

Mary Granahan (née Prendergast) was born and bred and lived all her seventy-something years in Garston. She was a solidly built lady, greying hair always neatly permed, a strong, resonant, hugely pleasant tone of voice who, like Peggy, couldn't abide fools and 'people who acted the goat'.

Round faced with spectacles, round (but far from fat) body, she had a younger sister, Sally, who was tall, thin, fair, light on her feet and walked quickly, didn't wear spectacles, and didn't look anything like Mary. Sally got married in her forties, had a daughter, who immediately became one of childless Mary's great prides and joys. The others were her house and Uncle John.

Both the front room (everybody called it the parlour), but especially the back room, were scenes of the most wonderfully organised clutter. Every inch of floor space, with (almost) designated walk-ways, was covered with something or other: tidy stacks of magazines, apparently randomly placed puffs, standard lamps and small tables of varying sizes and heights and shapes, on which statues and bells and photographs and unspecified paraphernalia rested in the most intriguing anarchy. At any given request, Mary magically knew exactly where to put her hand on any of the innumerable objects in the room and tell the story behind them.

Of course, walls and fire-grate were not exempt. There were photographs large and small and medium sized on every wall so as to make wall papering or painting largely unnecessary. Over the fire place was a huge portrait of The Sacred Heart. Though Mary was very openly critical of priests in general and Canon Henry Moffat in particular she considered herself – and was, by any standards – what we called a 'good Catholic'.

Without fail, they'd both be at eight o'clock Mass every Sunday morning, gave weekly when the Canon came collecting for the Altar Society, went to Novena on Wednesday night, whatever the weather, whatever the season. When priests came to our house, invited by my Father, to lure me away to some seminary or other at the age of eleven, thereafter to convert pagans around the world, preferably Africa, Mary let her contrary feelings be known. My Father didn't like her for that.

They were quite clearly utterly devoted to each other, though in a practical, easy going way, completely natural, like brother and sister rather than husband and wife: she, manifestly so, he, by the gentle way he looked at her and happily agreed with everything she said and did. And Mary, as intimated, was a woman of fixed and strong convictions, who always got her way in sixty-one, Otway Street. John simply never raised the slightest objection. He was an enormously contented man.

Uncle John was Scottish and had been born in Hamilton, and in spite of the fact that he'd spent thirty-plus years in Garston by the time I really got to know him, his accent remained incomprehensible to everyone but Mary, who often quite happily translated. Such understanding was complicated even further by the fact that he wore overly large false teeth which seemed intent on escape, with the result that he invariably spoke with a kind of whistle. But, like Frankie Jones, he was a man of immediate and immense friendliness, never, ever without a smile, which crinkled his features and partially closed his eyes, and a good word about everyone and everything. He worked in the Bobbin Works.

Whilst Mary was well proportioned, John was wiry and spare. Thin, sandy hair combed straight back from a sloping forehead, an oval face, like a bow from a side view. Large ears, lively eyes, an easy smile.

I have an early photograph of him supporting Anthony and me on the window sill of number sixty-three, short sleeved, knitted pullover with rows of colours, long sleeved shirt with cuffs carefully rolled up beyond his elbows.

John loved Scottish music, and we frequently heard Jimmy Shand through the wall that separated our two houses, heard and felt John keeping time with a heavy foot. I remember us buying him Andy Stewart's 'A Scottish Soldier' in the Christmas of 1961, and he must have played it until the groove was worn through.

One day, a Sunday, I do remember – I don't remember the season nor the year, but I was probably no more than eight years old – I was playing noisily on the landing of the stairs. My Father was out somewhere:

probably Third Order at Saint Anthony of Padua's Church, Mossley Hill. Half way down the stairs was a child's tin of paints that I'd left there. I had numerous interests, and colouring books was one of them. Stamps, too, all neatly in place in my Seven Seas album bought at Cyril Ainsworth's, with Turkey, Thrace and Uruguay all following each other.

As I came down the stairs, I stood on the flat tin of paints, my feet went from under me, and I crashed to the bottom of the stairs, dislodging the tin, which split open and the edge cut me deeply in the fleshy part at the very top of my leg. My left leg.

Well, there was blood everywhere. My Mother probably screamed, panicked, ran to Eileen's – Frank was at the loft with his pigeons – banged next door at number sixty-one.

Mary swaddled me in make shift bandages and good towels and spare bed sheets in an attempt to stem the flood of copious blood, while John ran up the street and into The Lane. He saw the sixty-six bus just leaving its station at the bottom, bound for Woolton and Belle Vale, Gateacre, waited for it to stop outside Joey Cooke's house, told the driver to wait. Ran back for me, a bloodied bundle, carried me to the bus. Told the driver to stop the bus at Garston Hospital gates. Ran up the sloping driveway to the front door, shushing my cries and fear. Waited all Sunday afternoon and evening with me until they'd painfully stitched me up.

Almost sixty years later – sixty, Jesus! – the scar's still there. I'll show you if you're in any doubt as to the truth of the story! Left leg, right at the very top, the fleshy part! Honest to God!

3. There's only one Miss Murray

Holy Tripe was the first school I ever attended. You won't be remotely surprised to know that that's not its real name, of course; but for most of Garston's non-Catholics – without malice – and for many Catholics, too, that was the name generally given to Holy Trinity Roman Catholic Junior School, situated on Banks Road, Garston, Liverpool 19.

In much the same way, we Catholics referred to all non-Catholics of all shades and shapes as Proddy Dogs, again, in the main, without too much malice (though some did have an issue, perhaps, with the Orange Lodge and its processions up Window Lane around Sunday lunch time).

Nowadays, of course, we'd all be up in front of the Race Relations Board or Quango or something equally pointless, asked to explain our lack of political correctness. Or something.

If you come up Window Lane from The Cast Iron Shore, turn right at the very top – otherwise you'll end up in The Gas Works, and you wouldn't want that to happen, would you! – go along Banks Road for two hundred yards or less. Banks Road Church of England School – an uninspired and less than inspirational name – is on your right. Beyond that is Top Park, where we had what passed for organised school games, tree trunks the natural goal posts, kicking a leather football with the consistency of lead and running around in headless chicken fashion.

Just slightly beyond is where Kevin Harmon – or was it Desmond Taylor? I can never quite remember – was knocked down by the 80A bus, crawled from under it, and lived to tell the tale. His mother gave him a good hiding when he got home for making a show of her all over Garston: in those days, mothers felt such a responsibility incumbent upon them. And a little further to the right, behind the bowling green, lived Idris Hughes and his wife and his precious, precocious children.

Across from Top Park is the Church of Holy Trinity, where Canon Henry Moffat, and, later, Monsignor Cyril Taylor (late of The Metropolitan Cathedral of Christ The King) and handsome Father Thomas Butler, reigned supreme for what seemed countless years. Up the side of the church, on your left and barely visible, The Cinder Path rises narrowly until you come to one of the three entrances, of sorts, to the school playground; then across the yard to the main entrance of the building.

Theoretically, at least, you could get to the same destination by using the Priests' Path on the other side of the church. But woe-betide you if Joe Whelan – caretaker and one-time footballer, photographed in Argentina (of all places) in 1935 – caught you. His wife was a gentle, slightly nervous woman, and daughter Elizabeth, too, a lovely, uncomplicated girl, married and divorced young, but still a lovely girl. We'll leave our Stanley for another day, shall we? But Joe was, to us kids, a miserable, unsmiling sod, who tended to bark rather than speak. God knows how he treated his own kids.

Anyway, where we? Ah, yes, walking across the playground. That same playground that witnessed me bouncing on my head on my very first day at school. I recall rushing out at four o'clock, full of things to tell about adventures to anybody willing to listen, and Tony Forde, the bastard, put one of his feet judiciously in front of my careering four year old feet. I momentarily grew wings until I landed painfully on concrete. The result looked like a second forehead glowingly attached to my natural forehead.

Right, let's get back to the playground. Veer left a little – otherwise you'll end up in the air-raid shelters, where Geraldine De Reuter used to give out rationed kisses to her beau-of-the-week and became (some said) unnaturally shapely for one so young in years. Alternatively, you'll end up in the boys' toilets, which stunk to high heavens on anything approaching a hot day, and often overflowed. In fact, heat was no requirement: they always stunk to high heavens.

The school is a gaunt, featureless, parallelogram of a building, its sombre aspect somewhat relieved by classroom windows on both floors. Go through the front door into what would probably be called a reception area – except that there's never anybody there to receive you – and a further door opens on a fairly wide corridor, classrooms to right and left. Left of the reception-area-that-isn't you'll find Mr. Smythe's surprisingly small office, toilet and washroom alongside, the door always open, for some reason. It's your most earnest wish that you won't see his office from the inside looking out.

He's a big man, is Mr. Smythe. He always wears a dark blue suit, thin black hair combed back from his forehead, a very round face with a small, flat nose and small ears for such a big man, and he walks importantly and expansively. He rings the school hand-bell every morning to start school, and to bring the kids in from playtime and lunch break, and again for the start of afternoon classes.

He seems welded to his bell, striding from the front playground to the back playground, wincing, momentarily closing his eyes and shaking his head almost imperceptibly as he passes the boys' toilets on his way to call in the older children. They only know him as a ringer of bells. They are, the majority of them, unaware that he's a teacher. Actually, he doesn't teach: he merely administers the school of some three hundred children, and calls them Sonny Jim and Young Lady, which is a commendably Christian way of addressing some of them, given their varied pedigree.

He looks like a headmaster, and he talks like one, and not at all in the way that people from Under The Bridge talk. He's respected by the parents, or treated with respectful suspicion, and everyone tacitly admits that his word is final. He's got a good, authoritative voice, and he uses it well.

Down the corridor on the right hand side is Miss Coleman's classroom, and everybody in the world absolutely loves Miss Coleman, bless her. She's patience personified with the youngest class in Holy Tripe, all fifty-odd of them somehow packed into a classroom whose size would not be acceptable by today's standards, such as they are. She sings to them and tells them stories about Jesus and Mary, plays games and scripts little dramas, wipes the floor when the kids inadvertently pee, talks to the mothers in a fashion the mothers understand, somehow manages to love all the kids entrusted to her. To the shame of the nation, she was never publically rewarded, though she most assuredly went straight to Heaven,

Saint Peter waving her Inside without hesitation, his book full of her many achievements.

I remember she once briefly left the class to ask Mr. Smythe, no more than paces away, to come in here and "Just you listen to this young child, Mr. Smythe", who knew all his prayers by heart, could tell stories from The Bible and Jesus' life, sang every hymn that anybody could possibly wish to know for any feast you might care to name, knew all the Catechism answers verbatim (though she privately doubted that he could possibly know what they meant). That was me, aged four going on five, totally and utterly ignorant of nursery rhymes, but a budding cardinal, no doubt, to the manifest joy of my Father.

Miss Coleman called the children 'children', loved them all with signal patience, spent her whole teaching career at Holy Tripe, as far as I know. She lived in Gateacre in a cottage just before you got to the park, and got the sixty-six bus every day, dropping her off at The Gasworks' gate, just before it made the turn into Window Lane. She was never late for school, and was never absent through sickness. Miss Coleman was a saint, everybody said, and everybody was right. They don't make Miss Colemans any more: an unsung national treasure and proof, where needed, of the immense Goodness of God and His creation.

Next door – as a sort of counterpoint – was the loathsome Mrs. Quiggley (whose existence God must surely have to explain), and Mrs. Quiggley loathed me. Absolutely and ostentatiously loathed me, she did. Off and on, in desultory fashion, I've spent more than half a century wondering why she loathed me, and I'm still as ignorant now as I was then of the reasons for her naked hostility towards me. Maybe she got out of the wrong side of bed every day of her life. She very possibly loathed all kids, and I was a bit sensitive. Ha! As if!

But she was a horrible, horrible, horrid, horrid woman, utterly lacking in minimal patience and the milk of human kindness, God charitably rest her immortal soul. She had a spectacularly beautiful late-teenage daughter who sometimes helped her in the classroom. How she ever produced anything so appealing I'm at a loss to explain. You wondered why she ever chose to teach. Or to beget, come to that.

As far as I recall, she was friendly with Mrs. Thomas, a spare, hawk-nosed woman with prominent teeth who taught across the corridor from Mrs. Quiggley's classroom, and who was exceedingly fortunate ever to have been joined in holy matrimony. She passed on her genes to an ugly, wizened, little son, who spent most of his five years at Holy Tripe in his mother's class.

But Miss Murray, beyond Mrs. Quiggley's classroom, was utterly beautiful, both inside and out. Especially out. She looked like a very young Lauren Bacall, though she was to everyone – and especially to Mr. Riley – a hundred times more beautiful, a present-day Julia Roberts, you might say.

There was an ease and grace and perfection to everything she said and did. Dressed utterly becomingly in flowing, billowing skirt, cardigan, flat shoes. Hair fragrant and smiling face. She was an absolute dream and reminded me, in later years, of the heroines lauded in song by The Everley Brothers and Buddy Holly and Ricky Nelson and others lesser known in those wonderful years of long ago and far away. Pass the handkerchief, will you, Our Dennis!

In addition to Mr. Smythe, who never taught but ran the school and was in charge of ringing the bell – if you remember: just checking that you're paying attention, back there – Holy Tripe had two male teachers. One of them was Mr. Kelly. Mr. Kelly was, to all appearances, slightly gruff and not tremendously approachable, as they say, but he was very far from unpleasant. In all probability he was a very shy man.

Freckled and bald headed except for a monkish fringe, a moustache like a well trimmed yard brush under his nose, he was a bit of an artist, his giant-size paintings and drawings – mostly of football scenes – gracing the walls of his classroom. Whenever he was engrossed in his new artistic oeuvre or momentarily out of the classroom, he'd appoint one of the kids to write the names of other children on the blackboard, under the headings of 'good' and 'bad'. And Heaven help any monitor who wrote down Bimbo Riley's or Jimmy State's name under 'bad'. Jimmy State, a child of immense, natural menace at the age of nine or ten, inspired naked fear. I frequently shat myself merely thinking of him.

Upstairs was basically one huge space, bound in on its four sides by the outer walls of the building, and was multi-functional, though that's not the sort of word that was in vogue in the 1950's. At either end of the space were huge, black-grey curtains, suspended well above head height, and behind them two classrooms. The larger area between the two classrooms was The Dinner Room, sometimes used when the nit-nurse held brief court, and generally overseen by Mrs. Carter, a small, rubber-faced woman with an immensely long ponytail wrapped many times around her head and above a stern face. She was ugly: there's no charitable way of saying it in any other way.

(Look out of one side of the classroom windows and you'll see veritable 'cordilleras' of coke in The Gasworks, almost, it seems, within touching distance. On the opposite side, a view of The Matchworks playing fields, and the aerodrome beyond that, where Childwall Uncle Frank loaded the bombers during the war, few of which ever came back. He never talked about it, even to Auntie Winnie, and he told her everything, normally. They were like two good friends rather than husband and wife.)

Mr. Riley taught in one of the impromptu classrooms, which remained impromptu throughout his long teaching career in Holy Trinity

Roman Catholic Junior School, his only school. Though we undoubtedly learned in his classroom our tables and how to write and a few other basic educational necessities, 'taught' strikes me as something of a misnomer, given the demands of my own (much later) teaching career, when short sleeves and perpetual motion seemed to be the order of the day. I seldom remember Mr. Riley standing up in front of his class of fifty snotty-nosed kids and actually 'teaching'. He always sat. He never took off his jacket.

On Monday mornings, just before first playtime, he'd ask us to "Put your hand up, children, if you went to Holy Mass yesterday. Right. Those with your hands down, kindly form a queue at my desk. And the rest of you kindly get on quietly with your work." Then, in a whisper, he'd grill those who'd missed Holy Mass the previous day.

"You know it's a mortal sin, don't you, and you'll go to hell for all eternity. Is that what you want for your immortal soul? Well, is it?" Jesus! Strangely enough, no parents ever complained about his dubious methodology. They didn't then. They let the teachers get on with it, and no disadvantage came of it, even when he called us 'pie-cans', whatever that meant.

Mr. Riley was distinctly round-shouldered, sitting or standing, and wore a mid-green sports jacket with shiny brown trousers. Hair beautifully barbered, fingers a rich shade of yellow-brown, thanks to the copious amounts of Woodbines he got through. A single man who lived with his single sister. A handsome man, too, and he quite clearly thought the very world of the marvellous Miss Murray. Who, with a brain cell, didn't?

She'd sometimes, for one reason or another we weren't privy to, come up to see him, and we'd all be invited to "Please stand up, children, for our very welcome guest, Miss Murray", which we did. Adoringly. Droolingly. They'd talk quietly together, share some personal remarks, perhaps. He'd touch her ever so lightly on the arm and they'd gently move apart, smiling or laughing innocently in some wonderfully beautiful way beyond our understanding. I don't think he ever got over it when she left to teach elsewhere, and who could blame him! She was a dream, by any standards you care to name.

Briefly, on the rebound, perhaps, Miss Harmon, at the other end of the 'huge space', eventually became the object of Mr. Riley's renewed interest in womankind. From time to time he'd tell us to "Put your pens and pencils down, children, and sit up straight and we'll give Miss Harmon's class a surprise". And we'd launch into a well rehearsed chorus.

"Little Sir Echo, how do you do? Hello? ..."

And then a pregnant silence until we heard a shuffling at the other end of the building, and then we'd start again.

"Little Sir Echo, how do you do? Hello? ..."

And Miss Harmon's class would reply with a tuneful (sometimes tuneless) "Hello!", and this would go on for a few minutes more until Miss Harmon's solid steps could be heard approaching. She was a muscular lady of manly stance, strong facial bone structure, and a generally serious appearance. I hope she got married in later life.

Much the same as with the much missed marvellous Miss Murray, both teachers would celebrate the joke and enjoy the moment, but you could see it wasn't quite the same, no matter how they tried.

Even we kids could appreciate that there was only one Miss Murray.

4. Ructions

"Can we watch the telly, please, Auntie Peg?"

We'd run down the back entry in the cold, wet darkness, Anthony and I, splashing through the puddles, past Dilworths' overhanging creeper that reached for the entry floor, knowing by instinct and use where to take longer than usual steps where the paving slabs were irregular and broken. 'Six-Five Special' was on.

There was no lock or latch on the back door, and when we went through Peggy was on her way to empty the tea leaves down the toilet at the bottom of the yard. Bronco, a malicious, malodorous, ill tempered, little shit of a Corgi of some considerable age and dubious pedigree, was in the corner by the dustbin, sniffing delicately before painfully cocking an ancient leg to wet.

Directly to the left of the back door as you came into the yard was a battered old door which was lying on its edge, forming an angle with the floor of the yard. For two years or more Dennis had used it as a hutch to keep a rabbit he'd found at the bottom of King Street. One afternoon, he came home from school and had to climb over the wall to get in. The back yard door had a lock on it then, for reasons I can't remember. The expected happened. He fell off the wall onto the angled door and squashed the rabbit. Buried it with fitting respect and solemnity down The Shore that same evening, me trailing dutifully behind him.

On summer days, during the long school holidays, when Peggy was at work, Dennis and I gave puppet shows in the back yard – his idea, of course – charged a penny entrance fee, and provided jam bread and dandelion and burdock pop in half a dozen cracked old cups. Peggy surely suspected something but never got to the bottom of it. After a long day in the machine shop, detective work was the last thing she had on her tired mind when she got home. She was barely ready for the nightly bingo at The Empire. Some nights she only went out of long tradition and loyalty.

But Violet Spenser and the rest of that brood; Norman Dixon (whose mother couldn't stand the sight of Our Dennis because, as old as she was, she couldn't best him in an argument); Georgie Darnell, curly headed, prescription spectacles on the very tip of his always running nose; Arthur Siddall (who became a vicar); Steven Kenny, with his gammy left leg and painful stutter; and various others – they all had a nice afternoon in Dennis' back yard, and they'd be gone, of course, before Peggy got home after five.

To the right of the back door were Georgie's empty 'pop bottles' all in a row, a balding brush of great age, and a mop that had seen much better days. The floor of the yard, with its many cracks like natural crazy paving, was gradually greening over with the wild things growing in complete indiscipline. The coal shed shared a wall with the outside toilet.

"Yes, love. Go right through if you like. I'm just making a cup of tea before the bingo. But don't wake up your Uncle George, for God's sake".

The heat of the sitting room smothered us like a blanket. They were a far from rich family, nor would they ever be as long as George took it into his head periodically to spend a significant proportion of Thursday's wages on a few drinks – he jokingly called them 'pop' – and the horses.

In all his many years at Simpson's – trilby, long, brown mackintosh almost reaching his ankles (Simpson, not Uncle George) – George had never made a profit on the horses. On the very few occasions that his horses won, a rare event, he told Simmie to put his paltry winnings on the favourite of the next race, whatever that might be. George only ever backed the favourites.

But in his own way, he was philosophical about his losses: he had this tremendous ability to bounce back in the belief that better times were coming, were just around the corner. Either that, or he forgot about the losses, refusing to let them affect him adversely. In many ways, Uncle George was a remarkably uncomplicated man.

In spite of all this, Peggy had the house decorated and furnished for what then passed as good taste: ankle deep carpets, armchairs you'd get lost in, clusters of wall lights on every available wall. She preferred to pay by weekly instalments, in the sure and certain knowledge that the new item would wear out before the term of payment came to an end. And, of course, it was Peggy who paid for everything. So, on those odd occasions when George came home the worse for wear – as now – all her bills and the long hours at the machinists' table working to pay the bills flooded back to her in bitterness and frustration and tears.

"Why the bloody hell should I pay for the rotten things when there's a man in the house. Good-Jesus-Tonight, Lizzie, he must think I'm made of money. The get, he is!"

George was lying on the sofa, quite clearly in another world. There was a slight but persistent smell of sour alcohol when he breathed out noisily and fitfully. He seemed to be at peace, which upset Peggy even further.

"Makes a show of me, the swine's get!"

But the swine's get went on snoring and slobbering, oblivious, in his untroubled slumber, to everything going on around him. He was lying on his back in his stocking feet, heavy, formless jeans, and a pullover of indeterminate colour. He hadn't shaved that morning since there was no work on Garston Docks, and he'd gone straight to The Woodcutters at the bottom of The Lane after signing on.

When Peggy got in just after five-thirty, she'd found him on the floor where Puddin English had dumped him at closing time, still dressed in the overcoat Peggy had bought from Jimmy the Jew a few Christmases ago. It wasn't the first time he'd arrived home in this fashion, and after a bout of hysterics, when first the cat, then a surprised Bronco, for good measure, had been kicked out into the back yard, she realised something she was already aware of: it wouldn't be the last time. Yet, in spite of fitful appearances to the contrary, it was strangely a marriage of some meaning and duration. That Georgie ever reached his seventies was a minor miracle in itself.

Peggy was short and thin, not a picking on her, always wore nice clothes and seemed to totter on abnormally high heels, her face sharp and pale behind enormous black spectacles, and she was possessed of a naturally clear, distinctive voice. Throughout her entire life – she died when she was ninety – her hair managed to remain jet black. Another miracle!

She couldn't stand fools nor people who "acted the goat. I've got no time for them sort." When Eileen had one of her periodic rants of jealousy over something or other, Peggy would walk away with "Oh, I can't be listening to this Eileen. I've got better things to do with my time! I'm going home this minute."

My Mother and her younger sister often thought Peggy was a 'funnyosity', but the fact of the matter was that she was direct and uncomplicated in a way they and others weren't, and told you the truth as she saw it. If you were sensible, you'd never ask Peggy what she thought about such and such because she'd give it to you straight, whether you liked it or not. She wasn't being awkward: you asked the question, you got the answer. Maybe not the answer you wanted, but a direct answer nonetheless.

And there's another thing: she didn't jangle about others. So more than once she'd fall out with my Mother or Eileen, both of whom, if the truth be known, were not averse to a bit of gossip. They weren't in Florrie Ellis' league, of course. Nobody was: she was a professional where gossip was concerned.

Every now and then, Mrs. Thomas, Peggy's mother, would stay for the evening. A tiny woman with a warm Irish accent, a whisper of a voice and a gravelly cough which made her sometimes gasp for breath, she was fiercely independent and lived by herself up The Village. That's probably who Peggy took after.

"Where's your Mum, love? In your Auntie Eileen's, is she?"

We nodded, hoping she wouldn't ask too many questions, but she continued as she got ready for the bingo, walking from the kitchen to the dining room and back again.

"Your Dad gone to work, then, has he?"

"Yes, Auntie Peg."

She busied herself, moving things inconsequentially from one place to another, and hummed a tuneless tune (just about recognisable as 'Hushaby, little guitar', her current favourite), all of which, from past experience, indicated that she wasn't going to let the conversation end without a fight.

"Your Auntie Eileen's been down."

Pause.

"She said there was a priest. A German priest, she said."

His name was Father Josef Werner, a Divine Word Missionary Priest, arrived from the house in Gateacre on the 66 bus. He was indeed German, but he was very nice, even if he did stay for hours on end. My Mother was never quite sure what to do with him, especially as his command of English left something to be desired, and much the same conversations were invariably repeated week after week, losing their spontaneity in the bargain. They talked a lot about the weather.

There'd been a Vocations Exhibition held in the vast fields opposite Bishop Eaton Monastery in Childwall, just off Queen's Drive, and the two Top Classes had been bussed there, boys and girls, the best part of one hundred, with their two teachers.

I came home with an armful of brochures: The Divine Word Fathers, The White Fathers, De Monfort Fathers, The Jesuits, Franciscans, Benedictines, Redemptorists, Dominicans and many more I can't now remember. An armful of brochures was obligatory in our house, and I was under orders to bring home as many as were available so that I'd have the widest choice of options for when I started converting heathens in Africa (or South America, at a push). Under my bed rested The Mission Box, which would pay for my education with whichever order of priests was selected for me. Mary Granahan's brother, 'Our Phil', always said you should let your lads go to one of those places, the seminaries, until they were sixteen or so: they'd get a first class education, then you could take them out and they'd get a good job.

(Years later, Bartomeu Barceló Roig, that lovely, lovely man, easily convinced my Father that I was a tailor-made priest, got me as far as three weeks staying in the then isolated Monastery of Lluc, Mallorca – one bus a day, one post a week, cold water showers every day – almost made a priest out of me. Fortunately, I escaped and lived to tell the tale. Fifty years later and Bartomeu bares no grudge: still writes to me regularly, God bless him. And me to him, God bless me.)

But Father Josef Werner came week after week after week following my Father's invitation, and my Mother fed him sandwiches and scones and tea while I was out with Our Dennis up at The Iron Bridge, collecting train numbers, Dennis positioning himself in such a manner that he could pee down at the train as it steamed and roared and belched beneath us, never once letting up, never once flinching until the train had passed or he'd exhausted his water, almost out of breath and choking, his pumps wet.

"So, what did your Dad say when he went out? When the German priest went out the front door, what did your Dad say, then? Was he pleased, was he?"

"No, Auntie Peg, he wasn't much."

"What did he say then? Your Dad, what did he say?"

"Well, he didn't say much, Auntie Peg."

"Are you sure, love? Are you sure he didn't? It's not like your Dad not to say nothing. What did he say, then?"

I shifted in the armchair, visibly discomforted. I hadn't expected that Peggy would know about the matter. Once she'd opened the topic, neither had I expected her to continue with such single-minded purpose, though that was typical of her.

"He said I was a little bugger, Auntie Peg."

Pause.

"Well, I'll go to the foot of our stairs. Just fancy that, now. "

Pause.

"Why did he say that, love?"

Pause.

"I went an' told him, the priest, I didn't want to be no priest any more, Auntie Peg."

She considered this a moment or two.

"And then what did he do, love?"

"Well, he went all wet round the mouth and said this isn't over by a bloody long chalk and don't forget it neither and then he went round the house banging doors and when he went out to work he forgot his sandwiches."

By now, Peggy had seated herself on the arm of the chair and placed the emptied tea pot in her lap, warming her hands and thinking how to go on from there: she had no intention of leaving the story hanging in the air. She looked long and hard at me as if lost for words, and, realising this, I readily obliged.

"Only, he came back almost straight away an' snatched them up an' when he was going out he said I was a little bugger again. There were ructions."

She made no further comment. Nevertheless, long stares and thoughtful glances in my direction, the shaking of head and furrowing of brow and pursing of lips, accompanied by sniffs and other such signs of bewilderment and lack of understanding, all indicated that the matter was still very much on her mind.

Finally, as if all were beyond her comprehension, she pursed her lips again and got up and went into the kitchen, banging a few pots and pans, reminding herself to tell Ruth Glennon all about it at the interval.

"If your Uncle George wakes up," she said, coming back into the by now sweltering sitting room, "tell him where I've gone, will you. I'll leave this packet of cigs here for him, but I don't think he'll wake up for quite a bit yet".

And with that, she shot him a look that would have withered any conscious mortal. George remained blissfully unmoved, his mouth open, quietly, contentedly spluttering.

She put two pencils in her bag, one for herself and one for Ruth, and stood in front of the mirror over the roaring fire, a cigarette dangling from her mouth, smoke in her eyes, combing her hair more with her hands and fingers than with the steel comb.

"And if Our Dennis comes in, tell him I've left him some salmon sandwiches in the back kitchen".

"All right, Auntie Peg".

She went over to the snoring George, scowled at him, stepped over Bronco, and passed between the two armchairs on the way out.

She slammed the front door – if you didn't, it wouldn't close properly: George didn't stir – walked through the entry into Shakespeare Street, dark and wet, miserable shadows in the cold, blustery night. She thought she had about five minutes to spare to meet Ruth and get to the bingo at The Empire on time.

And she had a story to tell Ruth.

5. Dream on, dream on, Teenage Queen

For eight long weeks and two days in the late summer of 1956 I simply adored Paula Winkles, to the extent that she filled every fibre of my ingenuous, impressionable being. I was twelve years of age and Paula was thirteen.

She wasn't truly beautiful in the conventionally accepted way, and even I knew that. Her eyes were full and round and always alive, her nose had a distinct bridge, and her mouth was pronounced, with fine, regular, chiselled teeth which you always saw when her mouth wasn't other than tightly closed; and when she smiled or laughed, everybody smiled or laughed with her and felt warm and vital and thoroughly worthwhile. Her hair was parted horizontally just above her hairline with the result that a fringe played lightly like gentle feathers on her forehead.

What most attracted me – and subsequently scores of others of both sexes – was that ineffable wholesomeness she unknowingly possessed: the ease and poetry and cleanness and naturalness of her movements, fluid and elegant, eloquent and utterly natural.

She ran like a boy yet effortlessly retained the elegance and attractiveness of a female. She ran unrestrained, yet with consummate grace, with exquisite smoothness. She ran and she raced against boys of all ages, and she eased past them and beat them, and she was happy for it, and they were happy for her, and nobody ever bore jealousy of her gifts.

She seemed to thrive on the company of boys, not in any promiscuous or questionable way, not a flirt, but with all the naturalness which appeared so much part of her very essence, and of everything she was involved in.

She lived with her parents and sister – two years younger and fairly portly, in comparison – on the Hollywood Estate. It was a house owned by the Corporation, but Mr. Winkles had given it a character which showed off his talents to best effect: a neat fence around, flowers tastefully planted, a lawn well cared for. It was on the other side of Top Park, beyond the bowling green and the tiny public library, where the 80c bus turned around and stopped for ten minutes before its return journey to the Pier Head. It didn't go as far as Speke.

The Hollywood estate was a place people spoke of with a certain respect and awe, a place they would have liked to live themselves, bathroom and toilet, three bedrooms, out of sight of the Gas Tank and The Bottle Works, and Bryant & May. There were even a few householders who boasted of the ownership of a car, parked neatly at the kerb, an Austin of England, maybe, or a Morris Minor. Pat Fitzgerald lived there. Pat liked me: she told me so, frequently, in Mrs. Quiggley's class.

I got to know Paula and her magical world completely by accident. For months and months I'd been dying for a bike, and one day, running a message for Eileen, I collided with the butcher's lad coming out of Woodson's, next door to Jack Corffe's on Window Lane, wheeling his laden shop-bike through the double-leaf (but still too narrow) doors.

Naturally, I'd seen him around before, and I knew he was at most two years older than I was. Despite that, he never seemed to go to school, but to all intents and purposes spent all his time delivering orders and helping in the back of the shop.

Like most shops in The Lane, it was small in size and could cater for no more than six or seven people at most at any one time. Like Jimmy Lunt's, its walls, from floor to ceiling, were full of food items and tins and bottles and packets. It was next to Waterworth's and Esther's and old Grandad Darlington, mending shoes in her back yard on his last, hammering nails into wood, cutting and planing and sawing and polishing, a drip on the end of his nose in all weathers.

"I want one like that."

"Like what?"

"Like that. That bike of yours."

"It's not mine. It's theirs, but they don't seem to mind if I take it home with me at night. See, if I have it at night, I get in quicker in the morning, like."

"It's great. Wish I had one."

He then assumed the pose of a man of property and noticed, apparently for the first time, that the mudguards were dusty, so he bent down and gave them a proprietary wipe with his open hand.

"Any road, me name's Tommy. What's yours?"

I told him. He didn't look overly impressed, but when he said I could have a ride some night if I wanted to, I told him that would be great. I knew roughly where he lived, but I didn't see how I'd be allowed to go that far from home on any evening. My Mother equated safety with the utmost proximity to home, and beyond Top Park and the library she always considered far too far away.

Late one Friday evening, warm like all summer evenings then, the air gentle and the high sky irregularly furrowed with wisps of white clouds, I was on my way home from an altar-boys' meeting with the Monsignor and Richard Ashcroft, Dick's lad, who later briefly became a priest. Instead of the normal way home, I accidently on purpose strayed across Top Park – bald patches punctuated irregularly by outcrops of wild growing grass – and it was there that I met Tommy for the second time.

"Haven't seen you for a long time. Thought you were coming over for a go on me bike, like."

I climbed on, put one foot on the ground to steady myself, flicked the peddle up for the downward push, and moved away from the kerb. It was a heavy bike, cumbersome and ugly, its steel baskets fore and aft, but I moved off slowly and in control. Even Tommy nodded his head in tacit approval.

"You can ride it to our house, if you like. Just past the library, there, then just around the corner. Go on, then."

(Like many shops in Garston, the public library, too, was a very small building, little more than twice the size of a normal front room in anybody's two-up-two-down house; and since bookshelves, not unnaturally, and the check-out desk, took up a significant space, there was little room remaining to swing the proverbial cat. But it served its purpose.)

Tommy ran alongside me, and when we got to his front gate, I dismounted elegantly, rearranged my trousers and under-crackers, and handed him the bike. It was then that I saw this vision that was Paula Winkles.

There's very little I can remember of that first meeting, except that my mouth was dry from being open so long in amazement. My heart raced worryingly, though it had nothing to do with the ride on Tommy's bike.

Paula was wearing a faintly red-and-white-striped dress and the whitest of tennis shoes, and with what seemed to me effortless timing she was serving to her sister a dozen or so yards away.

"She's my girlfriend, you know."

When I saw the direction of his nod, indicating the girl later introduced to me as Paula Winkles, my little heart sank. The surname struck me, for a moment, as being oddly comical. I now closed my mouth since I was in danger of passing out, not having taken a breath for quite a time.

"Not just mine, though."

"Eh?"

"She's not just my girlfriend. She goes out with loads of kids, like."

It was only later that my immaturity was enlightened by the explanation that 'going out' meant little more than the fact that she was friends with other lads. I was partially relieved. If I spoke to her on that first, fleeting meeting, I can't remember the details.

Thereafter, whenever I could, I went everywhere via Top Park, stopped at the library on the corner, smoothed down my rebellious quiff with spit, and nonchalantly, naturally, and scared stiff I went down Paula's road.

From that moment of meeting, my life for the next eight wonderful weeks and two days became one long subterfuge. My Mother became vaguely aware that her eldest son had acquired a sudden and inexplicable interest in aviation; that the aerodrome had lately become the centre of his very existence; that he had even acquired a small notebook where he recorded the times of arrivals and departures of air traffic. All of it utterly fictitious, of course.

She said she had to confess that she'd never even suspected that our war-time (and now largely defunct) aerodrome was so important or busy. Thankfully, she knew nothing whatsoever about aeroplanes – too many much more mundane things called constantly for her attention – otherwise she might have frowned and questioned the dozens of Illyushins and Fokker Friendships and Tupolevs which filled the pages of my notebook.

I worked hard, very hard indeed, at these lies, and my Mother, though confused, seemed happy with my explanations, glad that I'd found an interest that kept me busy during the endless summer.

And I'd happily sit at Paula's gate and watch her, enthralled by her movements and her grace, and by what I regarded as the very pinnacle of female beauty. On warm, gentle evenings, I raced her round the block on Tommy's delivery bike, but she, on foot, always won. Even now, I seem to recall taking the conscious decision never to beat her, and I rejoiced noisily at her athletic conquests.

When she had a turn on the bike, or when she handed me her tennis racket, or when she took the ball from her adoring ball-boy, I'd always leave my hand a little too long and brush hers, very gently, and that was enough.

And we'd talk about music and I'd pretend to have heard of Buddy Holly and Eddie Cochran and Johnny Cash and Bobby Darin, and Tommy would sing 'Dream Lover' completely out of tune, snatches of the lines drifting on the evening breeze as he whizzed by on his bike, head back and legs out and off the pedals.

And in that manner the unforgettable summer of 1956 went on.

I became something of a fixture at Paula's gate. Sometimes we'd walk – Paula and Tommy and me, and sometimes her sister – the short distance to The Cast Iron Shore, and sit and listen to the waves gently shushing against the unseen beach below.

I thanked God for giving me life and asked Him to bless Paula Winkles. And when I told her in passing that I was going off to Ireland the following week – the annual pilgrimage to Bath Avenue and Sandymount to see Dora and Bobby and Gerald and Mary and Uncle Jemmy and the rest of the tribe – I did so with the most acute regret, envisaging the end of the world as I knew it.

"I'd rather be here with you."

She looked at me, frowning and smiling, but mostly frowning, and told me I wore my heart on my sleeve, and I wondered then what she could possibly mean.

But the two weeks somehow came to an end, and, my exile over, my mood brightened miraculously on the last day of travelling, this in spite of the fact that the crossing had been rough and I spectacularly vomited on every square yard of the Queen Maud's upper deck. A seaman brushed the offending mess over the side.

To this day I remember nothing of Bath Avenue and Sandymount that year, nor Blackrock College, where I was to meet the unforgettable Bartomeu Barceló Roig three years later. Of course, my first call was to see Paula, and, embarrassed, to give her the pendant I'd bought in Bray on the first day in Ireland, secreting it in my Y-front underpants for the next fortnight. (I had more than one pair, just in case you're wondering.)

"It's for you, Paula." I seldom spoke her name directly to her, but my adoration was close to breaking point.

"Why did you do that?"

"I just did, that's all."

"It's quite nice. Thanks."

Her meagre gratitude meant much to me, and in my immature mind its giving somehow associated me with her, gave me a small part in her magical life. And on his way home that night across Top Park in the growing darkness, a late walker and dog might have seen a twelve year old boy skimming over the irregular patches of grass, snatches of a song borne on the warm air.

"Dream on, dream on, Teenage Queen,

Prettiest girl you've ever seen."

That September, Paula went back to school earlier than the Garston child from De La Salle Grammar School, Carr Lane East, Liverpool 11, who spent the mornings moping and frustrated. Not even his avid interest in aviation could fill the gap: so much for the Fokkers. The afternoons, however, were different.

When my Father came home from night work, his old Raleigh became available and I managed to smuggle it from his shed whilst still leaving the covering tarpaulin in place to suggest its continued presence there. That bike was his 'life line', he used to say. He was fond of 'taking the bull by the horns' and 'going to the foot of our stairs' and such colourful turns of phrase. 'Life line' was another.

I rode up beyond The Lyceum – the scene of some former, unforgivably delinquent behaviour! – once falling heavily as the front wheel got stuck in the tram tracks, and down to Aigburth Valley, where I stood beside the high railings and wire mesh of the tennis courts, Sefton Park behind me, Queen's Drive and Liverpool College a stone's throw away. Paula, a team member, trained there every afternoon.

"Hi. What you doing here?"

"Well, I had the afternoon off and nothing to do, so …"

From Monday to Friday of that first week of September I spent every afternoon there, watching her grace and suppleness, entranced, and at four o'clock I rode to the 85 bus stop with her, proud and fulfilled and inordinately at one with all things in Heaven and on earth.

The tragedy, such as it was, was that in my blindness I failed to see the blindingly obvious, that her interest was less than mine, that eight wonderful weeks and two days were far beyond the time span of a one sided love affair at that tender age.

"Hi, Paula. How was it today?"

"Fine."

And that was all she said, with a smile and a slight wave, and then she disappeared from sight. I stood there while the world fell apart and lost all meaning. I stared at the school gate and ridiculously read the Latin motto on the crest, and felt sick. I rode home in a daze. I cried all the way home, but the wind dried my tears.

"What's wrong with your face, love?"

"Nothing, Eileen."

"Your eyes are all puffed up. Been crying, have you?"

"No. Got some grit in me eye on the Dock Road, that's all. And I've been rubbing it to get it out since."

"Well, you just sit down there and I'll make you a nice cup of tea."

A nice cup of tea, again: the remedy for every ailment.

6. Ivanhoe at Christmas

Childwall Uncle Frankie Burnett lived in Childwall, Liverpool 16. Though he was born and bred in Garston – at 69, Otway Street, in fact – he spent all of what is generally known of his adult and married life with Auntie Winnie, his wife of some forty years, in this rather privileged corner of Liverpool. (At least, it used to be. Nowadays, let's just say that things have changed a little, and leave it at that.) To be exact, he lived in Francis Way, which he always half jokingly said had been named in his honour. Frank had a high opinion of himself, and with no small justification.

The semi detached house had been built just prior to The War: three bedrooms, though one of them, referred to as the 'box room', was indeed not much bigger than a box, whilst the other two bedrooms were very small by modern standards and dimensions. Nevertheless, they were decorated and maintained to an impeccable standard, as you'd expect if you knew Childwall Uncle Frank. Alongside the 'box room' was the bathroom, gleaming.

Beneath the bedrooms was what you'd probably term something of a 'compact' kitchen – certainly big enough for a childless couple – and a single sitting room, going from the front to the back of the house, which was always neat and tidy and spoke volumes for the house's neat and tidy occupants.

Frank had designed a small front garden entirely given over to a self-managing rockery, which Auntie Win weeded on those few occasions when a weed dared to present itself. Frank inspected it in proprietary fashion from time to time, and saw that it was good. The garden at the back of the house was a veritable picture of symmetrical neatness and pride: a manicured lawn with stripes (so it seemed) of alternating shades of green, borders of flowers on three sides, seemingly constantly in bloom; and towards the far end of the garden stood the greenhouse, exhibiting – you'll be surprised to be informed – the neatness that pervaded everything to do with the property's owners.

There were trays of potted seeds and plants in various stages of growth lined like little soldiers on the shelves, whilst underneath, suitably out of sight and hidden by a gingham table cloth that hung from the lowest shelf to just short of the floor, were Uncle Frank's tools, free of soil or grass, rake, lawn mower and scratcher, all gleaming.

It was such an enormous contrast to the houses where people – we people! – lived in Otway Street, Garston, Liverpool, 19. Basically, all the houses, linked together in a block of fourteen, consisted of just four rooms: two bedrooms above; a front room (invariably called the parlour, if you had aspirations to a higher social calling) and living room below (which, in some houses, performed the further function of kitchen, though how on earth people managed I'll never know). There was a toilet in the back yard, no bathroom. Like a number of people on our block – ours, Eileen's, but not Auntie Peg's – a kitchen with a brick base and wood superstructure was added, but that was entirely at the economic discretion of each individual householder.

('Householder' is perhaps not the appropriate word to use since nobody, to my certain knowledge, owned his house in our block, nor the one across the road, come to think of it. We all paid weekly rent. Every Saturday mid morning, Miss Hughes, the owner of our block of houses, would come to collect the rent from each house. She was a very pleasant lady, soberly but expensively dressed, and she'd listen patiently to any complaints about the property, promising prompt attention to any imperfections or malfunctions, and she kept her word. People knew where they stood with Miss Hughes.

I have a very clear memory of the despair of my Mother when, not for the first time by any means, we had a leak in one of the water pipes beneath the sitting room floor and out into the kitchen. The floor was dug up, the pipes were exposed both to locate the exact spot and to allow the earth to dry out, as you might expect. It being Christmas Eve when the burst occurred, we sat with this trench in the floor, under the window, until the new year. Not a happy time to add to the usual tensions normally experienced in our house over Christmas.)

Now then, where was I?

Childwall Uncle Frank, and Auntie Winnie, who came north from London during the first year of The War, stayed and married Frank before twelve months were out. Never lost her accent, a bubbly personality, a kind word and thought for everyone without exception, an instant interest in whatever interested you. She saw goodness in everyone and everything, yet tragically lost Frank to a stroke barely two years after he retired from the Silk Works. Never complained, just silently and privately shed a tear on occasions, and adjusted somehow. Wonderful woman; quite exemplary.

On those very few times in the year when we kids would see them, we'd live for weeks and weeks before the event with barely contained anticipation.

George and Sammy you'll be acquainted with through these pages, since they are crucial to their chapters; Eileen you'll know in passing from random remarks made throughout; and much the same, though on a lesser level, about my Mother. But Frank – for a variety of reasons – left least in his wake, and not even his two brothers and sisters could tell you anything in depth about him once he got married. In almost every conceivable way, he was different from them: infinitely more ambitious and sure of himself, keen to push onwards and upwards, keen to know what we kids expected out of life. To us kids, there's no doubt he was something of a celebrity.

I have a photograph taken of him in his early twenties: a short man, immaculately combed hair, clean cut shirt, tie at exactly the right angle and in the right place, bespoke suit, lightweight and expensively cut, a face ready for the future, where he would most assuredly make his mark. He'd loaded the bombers during The War, but refused to talk about his experiences, not even to Winnie.

We'd all get the 66 bus to its terminus at Belle Vale, then the 81 to the Childwall Five Ways – my Mother and brother, Eileen and Sheila – two or three times a year, the anticipation high, our best clothes washed and ironed well in advance for the special occasion.

"I don't know why we have to go and get all dolled up to see our Frank and Winnie, Liz. Twice a year. Three times at most. They're not royalty, you know. Why the blazes can't they come and see us, that's what I want to know. Too high and mighty."

"For God's sake, Eileen, just leave it. The kids love going. You know how much they enjoy it."

"Maybe so. But anyway ..."

And when we'd both started at De La Salle Grammar School, in the late fifties, Anthony and I, we'd go in our school uniform because we knew Frank would like that; would tacitly appreciate the fact that we'd put on our best to visit him and Winnie; expected it, if the truth be known, though he never said as much.

There's photographs taken by Frank with his precious up-to-the-minute camera, me the tallest with my school cap at a ridiculously rakish angle, smarmy and almost sneering at the camera, Anthony, all angelic features, Sheila in her National Health spectacles and a heart shaped smile on her mouth, chubby cheeks. And there's one taken by the lake in Calderstones Park, Our Dennis there this time, posed with the utmost care for Frank's camera, published in one of the photography competitions in the Liverpool Echo. It didn't win, but at least it got a creditable mention.

But it was the Christmas visit we most looked forward to, the once a year event that really mattered, when Frank and Winnie would come down on the late afternoon of Christmas Eve, and presents would be exchanged.

For no reason I can clearly remember (and for a few reasons I'll keep to myself, but which entailed Eileen's desire to be in the limelight, shall we say, to be seen as the hostess), her house was always the venue, though any welcoming food prepared for the visit (you won't be surprised to know, if you've been following events elsewhere) was always and exclusively done by my Mother. Feel free to use your own judgement as to why this was the case.

The presents would have been wrapped and name tags attached weeks and weeks in advance, and at the appointed time we'd go up the back entry into Eileen's. Childwall Uncle Frank always wanted to know in advance what we children would most appreciate as a present from him and Auntie Winnie; so, from early November, we'd start to think about possibilities (though I, personally, had known my choice months and months previously).

Now, amongst a variety of magazines and newspapers and comics, Mrs. Parker used to get a weekly supply of Children's Illustrated Classics in comic format. These were much more sophisticated, of course, than The Sun and The Comet, The Lion and The Tiger (with Roy of the Rovers, the Beckham (and beyond) of the Fifties, and Blackie Gray at inside left, Tubby Morton in goal, and Pierre Dupont, a recent acquisition from some swanky French club to bring Gallic flavour and interest to Grey Britain).

She sold titles like 'Treasure Island', 'A Tale of Two Cities', 'The Man in The Iron Mask' and – my favourite of all – 'Ivanhoe'. I read and reread it until I knew the exact sequence of events, and the actual dialogue in the speech bubbles above the characters' heads; read and reread it until the pages were frayed and loosened and held together with sticky tape. So, as far as I was concerned, 'Ivanhoe' was the natural request.

From early afternoon, my Mother had been in and out of Humes' and Jimmy Lunt's and Mrs. Davidson's in The Lane, making sure all was ready for the visit; Eileen, not to be bested ("You're not going to show me up, Lizzie") made some effort to have everything in order at number 69; and later, Peggy and Dennis, and maybe George, if they could find him on Christmas Eve late afternoon, would be up the back entry for a fleeting visit, Peggy making no comments.

When the long awaited arrivals appeared, getting off the 66 bus half way down Window Lane, Sheila was dispatched to meet them at the door, all excited, and expecting something very special as the only girl in the family. ("Well, Liz, and why not?") Breathlessly, she'd burst through our open front door, say something barely intelligible containing key words – Uncle Frank, Auntie Winnie, Childwall, though not necessarily in that order, and delivered at speed – and dash out again, her message partially understood, if you were familiar with the possible context of the situation. And within five minutes, scrubbed and brushed and wearing what passed for our best, we'd troop into Eileen's, there to be greeted by our Childwall visitors, Uncle Frank having each of us "Stand up straight so's I can see what you look like".

Tea was passed around and cakes were served and the adults exchanged news of this and that; the fire blazed and the wind and rain battered the windows; every light in the house was on; the outside toilet recently blancoed; sweet sherry served and tasted and commented on ("God, Frank, you'll be getting me drunk, won't he Liz?"); Frankie Jones would come in soaked from being up at the loft with his pigeons, his bicycle clips still round the legs of his trousers, a smile on his face and a self critical joke about his appearance.

And then, of course, the presents.

My Mother had spent time and effort (with the little money at her disposal) in the selection of the presents for the Childwall guests. Winnie, as we'd come to expect of her over the years, was unstintingly grateful for whatever she received and would invariably tell us "You shouldn't have, Liz, but it's really very thoughtful of you. You must have gone to a lot of trouble. Much appreciated, it really is. Look, Frank."

And Frank would say it was very nice and look at everybody with a slight smile on his mouth, which invariably conveyed his muted thanks, and how nice it was to be here once a year, and we must see if we can come more often. And then the children would be handed their presents, and though it was not yet Christmas Day, this was a special and exceptional occasion, and Frank would like to see how much we liked what they'd bought for us.

Sheila would gush her thanks and breathlessly tell Uncle Frank that the dolls' house was exactly what she was hoping for, which was true. She'd talked about nothing else for at least six months prior to Christmas. We'd all watch as it was carefully assembled and the miniature furniture was placed in the correct rooms, and Eileen would look at my Mother with intense satisfaction on her face, and purse her lips. Anthony loved painting and sketching, was, in fact, very gifted in this direction, so his box of paints and crayons and sketching pad were much appreciated. He said so, quietly and with a smile. He never said much, then.

Then Frank would show him what he should do to get the best results, and Anthony, always quiet and respectful by nature as a child, would smile angelically. If I told you what Our Dennis got on any one occasion over those few years, it would be merely a guess, because the fact is that I can't remember. Go and ask him yourself. He'll oblige: Our Dennis has always been obliging, and he's an absolute mine of information.

Childwall Uncle Frank relished occasions like this – in so far as they were occasions, happening only once a year as they did – and he loved to be the benevolent centre of attention. So, he'd pretend that the present giving was over, make to look for his tea and cakes and Cornish pasties from Humes', then dramatically smite his forehead in mock remembrance that the ceremonies were not yet over for us children. He would produce a beautifully wrapped small package, and with a flourish he'd present it to me. We all knew, of course, that it would be 'Ivanhoe', but that would hardly lessen my enjoyment.

Slowly pealing off the expensive wrapping paper – smoothed out, it could be used for somebody else's present the next day – I opened the beautifully bound edition only to discover that there were no illustrations like the ones I'd so loved in the Children's Illustrated Classics, but rather tightly printed English with not a picture in sight.

I'm quite sure I managed to hide my acute disappointment. In my few years of life so far I'd pretty much excelled at this quality, having had many opportunities. Frank looked from one to the other of all those gathered in the small living room with a smile of satisfaction at his own achievement. Winnie, of course, added how she so much hoped I'd enjoy it, since she knew I was fascinated by the story of Ivanhoe, that most noble of noble knights.

Around nine o'clock, they caught the 66 from just outside Joey Cooke's house, and we all waved them off and wished them a Happy Christmas and a happy new year, with the hopes that we'd see them soon, knowing, of course, that we wouldn't. And then all the kids, except me, went to bed. I'd be one of the acolytes at Midnight Mass at Holy Trinity on Banks Road, coming home around one-thirty to mulled wine and mince pies, and then to bed, because I'd be required for the eleven o'clock Mass on Christmas Day.

I never did open 'Ivanhoe' a second time, nor did I tell anybody of my disappointment, convincing myself that when I was older I'd read it and understand it better. I didn't so I couldn't. But I do remember buying a new roll of sticky tape from Ainsworth's for my Children's Illustrated Classics edition of 'Ivanhoe', and I continued to read it avidly, as if every time were the first time.

I don't recall what Childwall Uncle Frank and Auntie Winnie gave me the following Christmas. I'm sure it was appropriate, and I'm sure I said thank you very much.

7. Mr. Moore and things on the floor

There was never any guile to Our Dennis, you know. You always got exactly what you saw with him. So when he knocked on Mrs. Ellis' front door one afternoon during one of those long, hot summer holidays of long ago and far away and asked: "Is your Nigger in, Mrs. Ellis?" he did so in total innocence, with not the slightest expectation that the severe physical consequences meted out on his person would be immensely painful, nor, indeed, that he'd said or done anything remotely wrong.

Mrs. Ellis leathered him there and then, to be followed by Peggy's equally painful version minutes later, much to Our Dennis's deep consternation and lack of understanding.

To explain: John Ellis was Mrs. Ellis' favourite son – in fact, her only son, since her other children were all females, tall, willowy girls, long dark hair, year-round natural tan. John was an immensely swarthy child, thick black hair (that never moved out of place even in the strongest wind), the brownest eyes you've ever seen, and remarkably pink gums, which stood out, so to speak, in the absence of most of his teeth, the result, some said, of a diet (if such is the correct word) of cakes and sweets and ice-cream, all on the grand scale. Mrs. Ellis couldn't bring herself to deny him anything. Even as a child he was, shall we say, incipiently chubby, and this inclination to fleshiness without the muscle to hang it on became more and more evident throughout his short and less than happy life, before he sky dived from a block of flats in Halewood. When you spoke to John there was a glaze in his eyes as if he weren't listening, a vacant smile with no indication of understanding.

Now, John's Granny, on his father's side, lived next door, and immediately beyond her in Shakespeare Street were the Loftus family with their four boys in a two-up two-down, no bathroom, outside toilet, bear in mind.

But the Granny, for some reason unexplained, preferred to live with her daughter-in-law – John's mother, if you've been following – with the result that the Granny's house was totally uninhabited. And this is where Our Dennis comes into it.

Dennis was what people in those days referred to as 'small for his age'. He invariably wore a woollen, short sleeved, knitted pullover – dark green with blue and black and white hoops, as I recall – under his liberty bodice because, Peggy said, he had a weak chest. But he could run like the very wind and was as hard as nails. From an early age he had no time for fools and time-wasters: he said they were "about as much use as an arse pocket in a vest". He also had a way with words, Our Dennis. Still has, if you must know.

An only child, him – though whether that's significant or not you'll have to judge for yourself – Dennis was always 'into things'. Not unsurprisingly, he immediately saw the possibilities of having Granny Ellis' house as his gang headquarters. At that particular time, the gang – a loose term, it has to be said, and mainly in Dennis's inventive mind – was comprised of the swarthy John, gullible Gordon Wass, me, and Dennis, who was self appointed leader and instigator of everything, from the totally innocent to the marginally anti-social.

Dennis spent one sweltering afternoon in his own backyard, making a set of membership cards for his gang which would give them entry into his Headquarters. But whatever slight chance there might have been that Granny Ellis' house would actually become gang HQ, where games were to be played, meetings held and future plans hammered out were put on hold on that hot summer afternoon when Mrs. Ellis reacted with such unexpected physical aggression.

Not one to be deterred by this outcome, Dennis turned his attention to chivalry. In one of his comics there had been a pictorial serial about The Knights of the Round Table. So, Dennis appointed himself King Arthur, I became Sir Lancelot, and Gordon Wass insisted on being Robin Hood, thereby unknowingly destroying the chronological unity of the enterprise. By this time, John Ellis tended not to join in anything very physical, and he was inclined to sweat more than what was generally deemed natural.

Our activities involved 'riding' up and down the back jigger, assailing any kids we met and requiring them to identify themselves, then repairing to our back yard, where we painted shields and visors and other necessary weaponry from the cardboard boxes Dennis mysteriously acquired from Esther's shop on Window Lane. Lances, swords and similar implements were taken, borrowed or appropriated from whatever sources came to hand.

Of course, you can only have a limited number of causes, can only kill so many Infidels and capture Jerusalem a limited number of times, so after a while chivalry was abandoned. The fact that Our Dennis shot Wassie in the eye with his bow and arrow might have had something to do with the cessation of hostilities. Mrs. Wass wasn't too pleased, so she and Peggy physically chastised Dennis in the now familiar manner. Dennis just sighed philosophically.

(And there was another hiding, too, and all for telling Eileen the truth, when he told her that "Our Sheila's goin' gozzy, Auntie Eil. Look at her left eye. It's looking at her right one!")

Lolly-ice sticks had a much briefer life. The idea was to collect and wash them, paint or crayon them with the gaudiest colours possible, and fix them via a nail to the handlebars of a bicycle or the front wheel. As you rode along, movement and wind encouraged the sticks to spin around, creating a kaleidoscope of colours. But since there was only one dilapidated bike between the three of us the activity soon lost its popularity, especially so when I flew inelegantly over the handlebars when I collided with an unseen lamp post in Saunby Street, painfully removing the skin from knees and elbows, afterwards inventing a story to explain my wounds so I wouldn't get a wallop. In those days, you got walloped for innocently inflicting self injury, the more so if you did something already deemed to be wrong in itself. Go figure.

Just opposite Elizabeth Whelan's house (and Stanley's!) there was a children's play area, enclosed by railings and two gates of entry. Apart from the normal swings and roundabouts, there was a jerker in one corner. Basically, it was a plank of wood suspended from two A-frame, iron structures, and you'd sit on it – it wasn't possible to stand – and jerk it back and forth with your own body movement. At a push – ahem! – it would accommodate four kids, and it was a potentially lethal plaything. One afternoon, Dennis and I commandeered it, and shoved off anyone who disagreed with us. We were pirates, you see, Dennis wearing what appeared to be a pair of Peggy's knickers on his head, a smear of soot on his top lip, and a patch over one eye, wielding a stick which was really a pirate's cutlass. I can't remember how I was dressed, though probably similarly: I invariably followed Dennis's lead.

All I do remember is the sensation of the jerker getting higher and higher and my own certainty that I couldn't hold on any longer, that I was going to be projected over the railings and into the road, or maybe impaled by them. My bowels started to move and my stomach made counterpoint noises, and I was sure I was going to die. Luckily for me, Dennis slowed it down by jumping off and somehow bringing it to a stop. In any case, he'd quickly grown tired of this latest project.

Collecting car numbers up and down Window Lane was another short lived activity initiated by Dennis, but since what few cars there were in those days tended to be the same week in and week out, something more exciting was sought by his inventive mind. Shortly after this, Peter Goosegogs was initiated into the gang because he had a dog.

Let me explain: his real name was Peter Ainsworth, Cyril's painfully gormless son. The original Ronnie Barker in 'Open All Hours', Cyril had a sweet shop on Window Lane, looking directly down Otway Street. Becca's fish-and-chip shop and Mrs. Davison's bakery and dairy were on either side. Cyril was a taciturn, humourless man, apparently only interested in the tiny confines of his shop. His wife, taller than he was, had a reputation for relative sophistication.

Peter was the youngest of the newly reconstituted gang of four but by some considerable way the tallest. The trouble was that he never seemed to know what to do with his arms and legs, and they kept getting in everybody's way. He had enormous ears which stuck out unnaturally from a head that looked as though it was covered with course straw, darting eyes which registered amazement even at the most mundane of events, and a large, wet, forever-open mouth over which he apparently had little control. Whatever he said had a habit of including present, past and future thoughts in constant collision. But he had a game mongrel called Bruce.

Dennis's idea was to construct a series of jumps, made from whatever materials came to hand, from the bottom of the entry (where Dennis lived in number 45) to Florrie Ellis' back yard door (number 67), just short of the top end. He then had the eager Bruce run the distance, to be verbally timed.

Peter was the first timekeeper (since Bruce was his dog) with disastrous results. He simply couldn't count in sequence when he got excited, so Bruce was awarded times that differed by as much as twenty seconds for the fifty yard dash over cardboard boxes and broken ladders placed on their sides. Interest was already on the wane by the time Bruce got run over in Window Lane, just outside Jimmy Lunt's, and hobbled on three fairly good legs for the rest of its days, though with something of a sideways movement.

It was around this time, I suppose, that Dennis and I started to bait Mackie, for no clearly definable reason, other than the fact that it seemed a good idea at the time. Mackie came from a very, very poor family. His mother would exchange her ration of butter for two packets of margarine, which would go further and last longer when it was melted a bit. She was a haggard, gentle lady, who, like many women in those bygone days, spent most of her brief life trying unsuccessfully to make ends meet.

At midday, we'd be out of Holy Trinity and on our way home down The Cinder Path. Coincidentally, Mackie somehow contrived to be there at the same time, and Dennis would go up to him and wordlessly stare at him for minutes on end from a distance of six inches or so. Disconcerted, Mackie didn't seem to know how to react, but after a few days something snapped in him and he grabbed Dennis by the throat, thereby lifting him off the ground.

From being a spectator, I became, as they say, a player. Seeing Dennis turning forty shades of red and purple and spluttering in Zulu, I kicked Mackie up the backside with everything I had. Screaming in pain, he released Dennis, who flopped to the floor breathlessly. Mackie, swiftly recovered, chased us across Banks Road and Top Park, along the back of Banks Road Junior School, down Derby Street and through the back entry into Window Lane, into Shakespeare Street, down the jigger to Eileen's, followed by Mackie's slapping feet and whatever missiles he managed to pick up in his pursuit of us, bouncing stones and bricks and pieces of wood off the back entry walls, sometimes off our heads and fleeing backsides.

Heaving painfully and sweating profusely, we'd wait ten minutes in total silence until we deemed the coast was clear.

This activity continued for a number of weeks. Mackie would wait for us in what seemed by now a designated place – the bottom of The Cinder Path – give us a start, and then chase us wildly home. Though he never actually caught us, it wasn't for his want of trying. We were daily terrified and terror gave us wings. Then, for no apparent reason, the whole thing suddenly stopped.

Like most kids of our age, we'd go to The Garston Empire for the Saturday matinee (no less a star than Gracie Fields once performed there in the 1930's!). We'd watch Tom Mix and Hopalong Cassidy and The Cisco Kid and the crusty Gabby Hayes, Gene Autrey and Roy Rogers (whose real name was Leonard Slye: no wonder he changed it, even if he did have a horse, Trigger, who once appeared with him and Dale Evans on none other than the stage of The Liverpool Empire) and other long forgotten cowboys, all very clearly well into advanced middle-age, ten-gallon hats that put at least a foot on their puny height, gun belts around portly waists that appeared to start just below their arm pits.

They'd kill Indians and other pesky varmints by the thousands, and although we were supposed to watch the goings-on on the screen in a civilised manner, we'd invariably participate in a variety of anti-social activities. The favourite pastime was to shower the screen – and everywhere else, for that matter – with whatever came to hand, or to career up and down the aisles whilst Mr. Moore and the other attendants strove with limited success to keep us in our seats, uselessly flashing their torches in search of the perpetrators.

Every once in a while, the projectionist would switch on the house lights to help the adults keep order. The second they went off, the din would recommence with a chorus of "Mr. Moore / Shit the floor / Wiped it up / An' done some more". And at the end of the performance, when the doors were flung open and blinding sunlight entered, we'd race down The Village to the traffic lights, to Elliot's, smacking our backsides like the goodies did to their horses, shooting everyone in sight. Oh, happy days!

At the top of The Village was another picture house, The Lyceum, a bit of a flea pit, if the truth be known, and not at all favourably comparable with The Garston Empire. Once in a blue moon, to vary things, we'd go there.

One late Saturday afternoon, and some time after the performance had finished, Dennis and I, on our way home, found ourselves down an alley at the side of the cinema. There was no preconceived plan to do it, but I recall picking up a stone and throwing it expertly through one of the panes of glass in what seemed to be a derelict outbuilding of the cinema.

Initial success bred further success, and a tacit competition ensued. I remember we'd happily broken all the windows when we were both unexpectedly seized from behind by the collar and dragged back into the cinema, from where the manager telephoned Heald Street

The policeman took us both home and sat us in front of our Mothers. My Father was actually working that day; God knows where Uncle George was. I remember quite clearly denying everything – absolutely everything – truthfully alleged by the cinema manager, who'd stayed at his post to ready himself for the evening performance after giving his (more than accurate) version of events.

Dennis said nothing at all, sitting open mouthed and incredulous as he listened to me swearing on everything imaginable, that it hadn't been us, that we weren't there, that the manager was wrong, that he'd completely fabricated the story, that he had it in for us, that we were as white as the driven snow.

More than fifty years later, I can't remember the outcome, though it can't have been unfavourable since my Father somehow never got to know and I don't recall getting the customary good hiding for anything. All I do remember is the utterly incomprehensible look on Our Dennis's face as I lied myself black and blue and somehow got us off: the look of recognition of a great injustice being done.

And more than fifty years later, Dennis is still much the same. Vastly more worldly wise, that's for sure, but still guileless in the nicest way, still completely honest, honourable and utterly straightforward.

You still get what you see with Our Dennis.

8. Pigeons

My Uncle Frankie Jones kept pigeons. Into his mid thirties, he suddenly decided he needed a hobby now that his daughter was growing up fast and clearly away from him (which didn't bother him too much), and had, in fact, long been the province of her mother (and more especially since mother and daughter invariably snarled at each other as their normal mode of contact and conversation: perfectly normal, if you think about it. Otherwise, they got on quite well, mother and daughter, except from time to time and without warning when Eileen erupted hysterically with "Don't start me!" her screeches heard as far away as King Street, and neighbours quaked in their very shoes).

He increasingly found he had little in common with woman, anyway: Frank didn't have the most minimal of wandering eyes, in spite of getting Reveille every week. So, in the early days of September, he joined night school classes up at the library on Bowden Road, having looked forward to it throughout the summer months. Something to do on long winter evenings after getting home from work, he thought.

Firstly, it was the guitar. He liked to listen to music, especially country-and-western – George Jones (no relative, of course), Marty Robbins, and Johnny Cash (of course) – and he often hummed the song or sang 'sotto voce' to it, except on Saturday night at eleven o'clock on his way home from The Mona Castle Public House, when his singing was anything other than 'sotto'. He particularly liked Marty's 'El Paso', thought Grady Martin's playing was brilliant, wanted to emulate him.

He'd bought a splendid looking guitar, twelve strings and forty shades of emerald green, shining magically in the light, unheard gems of music lurking deeply in its unplucked cords. Then he bought a tutor book. Quite consciously, he'd decided not even to strum his new acquisition – though the temptation was great – nor open the pages of the tutor book until the very night of the first lesson. He was keen, he told Eileen (who probably wasn't listening: but he told her, anyway) not to start off by teaching himself bad habits.

He dreamed of the music he'd play and the difference it would bring to the relative monotony of his life: of the acclaim of his family, of Stanley and Eric and Raymond and Charlie and his sisters. Maybe, at a push, Eileen might be impressed, though he was taking no bets on that one: it took a lot for him to get her undivided attention.

But on the first night his fingers were found to be ten thumbs, and his shame was deep when, in front of all the other aspiring Chet Atkins's, the tutor asked him why, if he were right handed, he held the guitar "in that rather unorthodox fashion".

Keen not to lose too much face, Frank continued to attend the lessons for the next four weeks, making hideous cacophony and having to replace the strings – all twelve of them within weeks – plucked with too much enthusiasm and too little art, and no small amount of increasing desperation.

In bitterness and deep personal disappointment, and with a feeling bordering on growing hatred for the instigator of his woes, Frank confined 'the bloody thing' to the back of the wardrobe, where its melodies slumbered unexplored, mutedly gathering dust.

With deep mental scars, but keeping his disappointment to himself, he privately decided to go his own way in this world. Night after night, after work, he studied the life and misdeeds of Alphonse Capone, borrowed from me and read 'In Cold Blood' in an eight hour sitting that lasted until four o'clock one Sunday morning, generally gorged himself on a diet of the American underworld and his boxing magazines – on Willie Pep and Carmen Basilio and Two-Ton Tony Galento, Archie Moore, and Rocky Marciano, of course.

And so might things have peacefully continued if Charlie hadn't asked him to do him 'a little favour'. Their Raymond had become depressed yet again, and needed Charlie's attention. Raymond was frequently getting depressed. And that's where pigeons came into the equation.

"Look, Frank, all I'm asking is for you to take over just for a few weeks or so till we get him back on his feet again."

"But I don't know anything about that sort of thing, Charlie. Pigeons, I mean."

"You don't have to, Frank. That's the beauty of it, see. There's nothing to know. You just let the little buggers out every morning and evening and sweep out the loft from time to time with an old yard brush, fill up the food and water ... and that's about it. Bob's your uncle, so to speak. Easy. Honest."

Frank frowned to indicate his less than total conviction, his lips moved, but no sound came out as he looked the proverbial picture of misery. He needed a cigarette.

"Look, Frank, it's only for about four weeks or so, see. Six at the most. You know how things are with our Raymond, and we've got to help him out. Things aren't easy for him, you know."

Frank knew, but he said he'd have to think about that one. Not about the business of Raymond, of course. Frank would have done anything for anybody, most especially his family, and they all knew they'd have to rally round Raymond from time to time. That was an on-going obligation willingly accepted by all of them.

In the evenings, he sat in his chair to the left of the roaring fire and paraded his life before him. He sensibly realised – because Frank was, amongst his many qualities, a sensible and sensitive man – that most alternatives demanded abilities he simply didn't have. Slowly, pigeons began to grow on him, so to speak.

"But what happens if they don't come when I whistle?" he asked Charlie, after nights of weighing up the proposition, his boxing magazines unopened on his knees.

"Who?"

"The pigeons. What happens then, then? I've got to be in The Matchworks for half seven, and I can't be standing round in the cold whistling me bloody head off while your birds fly around in circles and won't come in."

"There's no need."

"What d'you mean?"

"The birds know where they live, Frank. They've got a built in sort of radar for all that, see. They've got the instinct. You can take a bird hundreds and hundreds of miles from its loft, see, and it'll be as likely back home before you are."

In the week or so before he reluctantly took over, and still plagued by lingering doubts, Frank would stop on his way to work in the morning, get off his old bike, lean it against wall or railings, throw his head back, and, perforce, open his mouth. In this position, revolving on his feet, he scanned sky and trees and roofs and street lamps or any other places where homing pigeons might alight. In this position, he whistled to them in what he took to be a common language until he had to stop because he was starting to cough and splutter and get dizzy.

There then followed years of immense contentment and fulfilment for Frank. For a very long time he'd been accustomed to getting himself up at six every morning, making his own sandwiches (it had never entered Eileen's head that she might actually make them for him), and being out of the house long before wife and daughter confronted the questionable joys of a new day. To be up at the loft for about six-thirty, he reasoned, was asking very little more of him. He was basically a single man, in spite of being married.

The loft was situated on an eminence alongside The Alfred Jones Memorial Hospital (where Scottish Uncle John had carried me swaddled in blood-stained towels and sheets) and had views in all directions, except to the north.

Over there, over on your left, that's where the New Road will be when they eventually finish the road works that seem to have camped there for the last couple of years or so. Move your gaze right a touch and you can just about see the railway junction behind the supermarket and the banks and all the other shops of daily necessities.

There's The Empire Cinema over there, and The Village, Saint Francis of Assisi's Roman Catholic Church, where I met Stella Fitzpatrick at The Legion of Mary, a head taller than I was (Stella, not Mary), Harold Collins' Barber's Shop, and Frank's mother's house. All a fair distance away, they all are, so the sounds sometimes drift over to you, delayed, and people scurry about like ants. Further right, over towards the south, the railway lines emerge, cross the bridge, and disappear behind more buildings of varied shape and size and substance.

The Garston Wash House is just over the ridge there on your left, where my Mother pulled and pushed an old pram every Friday mid morning from Otway Street, returning out of breath, out of sorts, beetroot red with the heat and the work, half the load invariably Eileen's, her younger sister by seventeen years. I have to say that even at the best of times – whatever they were – Eileen would never do anything she could get my Mother to do on her behalf. My Mother was soft that way. I'd often tell Eileen so, and get walloped for my cheek. But it was a small price to pay for getting across my point of view.

The allotment was hemmed in by multi-vintage fencing that Charlie had managed to salvage from The Shore over the years, but Frank was undisturbed by its irregularity. Around to the left, and out towards the gate, and forming something of a maze in the earth, were paths which Charlie had made with old bricks of all sizes and description. What was not path Frank converted into a garden and planted potatoes and cauliflowers and cabbages, all of which he took to his mother's house.

Here, as he told them in The Mona Castle Public House on Saturday night, Frank was in his very element. Finishing work at five thirty, he always went directly to the loft and then home for tea (seldom a culinary feast: "What d'you fancy for your tea, then, Frank? I'll see if our Lizzie's made more than she needs"). But as weeks became months, he was never home before nine on summer evenings.

Sitting on an old beach chair in front of his loft, rolling his own, he breathed in contentedly, talked to his birds – they were his now: that was his unspoken assumption – and he called them by name, a pile of stones always at his feet for the approach of any reckless cat. And in winter, muffled up against the wind and the biting cold, a tarpaulin over his shoulders, peaked cap over his eyes, he moved briskly in the inhospitable darkness of mornings and rain slashed nights. The birds were never any trouble to him. He recognised them, he thought, like the shepherd recognised his sheep.

In the early days, Charlie made increasingly unconcerned visits, which soon stopped, as if some tacit agreement had been made over the transfer of ownership (even after Raymond got over his latest in a long line of bouts of depression), and Frank's only other visitors were other fanciers.

They told him about their little association, The Top Club, and how they'd be very happy for him to come and join them sometime. There were, they said, advantages to this, since they could buy feed more cheaply; could cut the cost of sending his pigeons away when they went for training flights or races; could do a thousand and one things for each other. Frank's initial keenness to maintain his own privacy and independence was soon overcome by the prospect of sharing all his free time with men who shared his passion. So, Saturday night became Frank's night out.

He shaved meticulously in the back kitchen, standing in his vest, trousers and dangling braces; washed his hair in the bowl in the sink, rinsing with near-boiling water from the kettle on the stove; dressed in his light green wedding suit which had lain all Saturday afternoon on his bed. Kissing Eileen on a cheek proffered with all the warmth of a royal handshake ("Enjoy yourself, love!"), he left the house, walked to the end of the block, cut through the entry into Shakespeare Street, down to King Street, and along to The Top Club.

His pint was already on the bar when he got there, and he waved companionably to new friends and old acquaintances. He played dominoes, and nobody cared who won; allowed himself to be pressed to another pint; unselfishly compared notes, offering praise and commiserations on victories and defeats and tragedies; and went home, promising, as always, to come back next week, inviting them up to his loft, "any time you want, lads". Smiling, he let himself in, sat for half an hour or so reading The Ring, groped and fumbled in the dark up the stairs, and slid into bed alongside Eileen.

Next day, he was up at the loft long before either mother or daughter had even contemplated rising. It was still brisk and there had been a moderate frost, but he loved the privacy of these hours, more private today since on Sunday few shops would be open, fewer buses would pass by, the only ones out and about being the church goers on their way to Saint Michael's or Saint Francis of Assisi. He'd stay there until midday, at least, go home for some dinner – always assuming Eileen had got round to preparing anything remotely edible – and go back for the whole afternoon and evening, whatever the weather.

He pushed his bike up the path at the back of the hospital and noticed places here and there in his perimeter fence that needed seeing to: that strong wind in the early hours of the morning, no doubt. That could be a job for this afternoon: a few nails here and there and it would be as good as new.

But he couldn't for the life of him remember leaving the gate that way last night. It hung awkwardly on one hinge, and when he got closer he saw the battered heads of cauliflowers and cabbages that littered the ground. It looked as though there'd been a stampede.

It was then that he knew beyond doubt that something else was wrong, so sure that he momentarily convinced himself that there was no need to look. He felt sick to the pit of his stomach, in the spittle in his mouth. He heard himself moan, and his hand went to his mouth. Good-Jesus -Tonight!

They were all dead. Every last one of them.

Slowly, unreally in control, he placed his bike against the sagging fence and moved to the door of the loft. How had he failed to notice, when he arrived, that it was ajar?

In spite of his sure premonition, he was unprepared for what he saw: the floor was an untidy carpet of bodies and feathers and blood and severed heads and feet and unnatural stillness. Unwilling to sully it further, he went outside, closed the door gently, and vomited behind the loft.

Then he went home to tell Eileen all about it, but she'd already gone out to The Empire for the bingo with Peggy and Ruth Glennon and wouldn't be back until after ten. He'd tell her then.

9. Sammy and the stuff of minor legends

I'm here to tell you from the very outset that I can't entirely verify every single item of what follows for the simple reason that it's the stuff of legends, either major or minor. Once the story is told, you'll surely agree, it becomes public property – no matter how private in the first place – as it's then coloured and shaded and reshaped and renewed or otherwise changed over the many years, depending on the whim of the story teller and his listener. After that, the listener becomes the next story teller, and Sammy's tale is a case in point, but somebody has to tell it: it's the very least he deserves, you'll come to agree.

Nobody said so in so many words, of course, but Sammy was undoubtedly the poor relation of the family whichever way you viewed him, though this was never in any way held against him, was never once given voice.

Uncle George, when in work and in possession of money – which wasn't often, if the truth be told, though he never complained – still somehow managed to be relatively prosperous in his own way, and by his own means, and thanks largely to Peggy's thrift and financial management on the domestic front.

Childwall Uncle Frank, by dint of uninterrupted work – something of a novelty in those days – at The Silk Works in Woolton had a nice house in a much sought after residential area of Liverpool 16. By these or any other standards of the day, he was an undoubted success.

Eileen never lacked for anything, thanks both to Frankie Jones – that lovely, lovely man, tragically gone before he was fifty – and to my own Mother, who treated her like an only child, getting everything she wanted at the first time of asking, which brought complications of its own. Even my Mother, in spite of everything, seldom counted herself an outright unfortunate.

But poor Sammy was, and it was his constant companion, though never once, to my certain knowledge, did he ever complain. You didn't in those days: it wasn't the thing to do.

My memory paints Sammy – if that's not too colourful a verb – in drab shades. His face was grey and lined, swollen and crumpled, with enormous bags under his eyes and his thick, unmoving hair, water-parted just off centre. Under a faded, frayed, formless gabardine mackintosh of indeterminate age and countless soakings, he wore a tie-less shirt buttoned at the neck, trousers that bunched at his scuffed shoes, hands clasped behind his back, fingers intertwined, round shouldered.

Just after The War, he married May Hargreaves, a woman who necessarily rationed her smiles and her laughter: life wasn't easy for her, either. They lived all their economically precarious life in Saunby Street, towards the bottom of The Lane.

My earliest memories, as faded as Sammy himself, were of his almost daily visits, for no clearly defined reason, to our house. In those days, the back door – and the front door, come to think of it – was never locked until you went to bed at night. I'd hear the latch being lifted and the grating of the door on the uneven floor of the back yard, then the kitchen door opening, and 'doo-dee-doo-doo', repeated times without number, minutes on end, which was Sammy's embarrassed calling card.

He'd stand there and hum tirelessly and tunelessly and answer my Mother's habitual questions about how he was, how May was, how Roy was, and Lyn, and she'd try not to make him feel any more embarrassed than he already must have been.

Sammy always brought with him a slight smell of wet clothing, and, on dry days, of cigarette smoke from his roll-your-own that he could just about afford, keeping the dog ends and recycling them in a little tin he always carried. My Mother would ritually offer him a cup of tea and he would ritually decline, saying he'd "just had me dinner, thanks, Liz", or that he was "just gonna have me dinner an' ah don' wanna spoil it, thanks any road, Liz".

My Mother and Eileen and George always looked sadly at him, wondering what might have become of him if it hadn't been for The War. Childwall Uncle Frank seldom saw him (but you shouldn't read anything into that: it was simply that their paths seldom crossed).

Up the back entries that paralleled Window Lane, he'd come, into Otway Street past Billy Davies' and Pye's houses on the corner, through the narrower entry between Esther's and Phillips', first left, and ten yards or so to our back door. Sometimes he'd bring Roy, a small, silent child, thin and flaxen haired, a wide, unsmiling mouth and expressionless face, impeccably mannered, his hand in Sammy's.

They'd stand there for what seemed ages, for no clearly apparent reason. From time to time, Sammy would give voice to a few inconsequential remarks in a thick Liverpool accent, something of a legacy of his experiences during The War. If it was raining, or if it was cold or hot, he'd make passing references to it in between lengthy bouts of silence, punctuated by more tuneless tunes, and then he'd say: "Well, I'm off, then. Come on, son. See you, Liz", and he'd be gone, and she'd follow him out, sometimes, up the back entry, and give him a two-shilling piece (which she herself could hardly afford).

He never once came for a hand-out, but in his embarrassment he was more than grateful for anything she surreptitiously gave him.

Sitting comfortably in a chair to the right of an invariably blazing fire, I'd wish him gone every time he came, not having the remotest understanding of his predicament nor the external forces – way beyond my understanding, and Sammy's, perhaps – that had shaped and misshaped his early life. Never once, then – through my ignorance and insensitivity – understanding the unkind fate that would accompany him throughout his sad life. Bastard, shameful thoughts, mine were then!

At barely eighteen years of age, young Sammy stowed away on Elder & Fyffe's SS Mopan, almost seventy men on board, no lifeboats, no minimal comforts, just the cold, immense, inhospitable Atlantic.

The practice, far from uncommon on Liverpool's docks in those days, was for groups of men to hang around the boat on the point of departure. Someone on deck might shout down the destination, and unemployed men, desperate for work of any kind, would swarm up the ropes thrown down to them, stagger aboard, and be gone for an indefinite period of time. That's what Sammy did, one October afternoon in 1940. Without telling anyone: there was simply no time.

SS Mopan steamed off to the West Indies, picked up a full cargo of bananas, and turned its face east, passing one of the many convoys from North America to war-weary Britain. Some five hundred miles off the west coast of Ireland, on 5th. November, 1940, the Kriegsmarine's Admiral Scheer ordered the captain of the banana boat to stop. All its crew was taken aboard the pocket battleship, which then sank SS Mopan.

The same Admiral Scheer, with Sammy and the crew on board, then proceeded to sink, amongst others, SS Beaverford, SS Maiden, and SS Fresno, with the loss of all on board each ship. Sammy and his relatively fortunate companions were transferred two weeks later to German supply ship Dix (flying the US flag, the cowardly sods), where they spent four long months in Dix's fumes-filled empty tanks, which undoubtedly was the start of Sammy's ill health over the next forty years or so.

Eventually, they were landed in Bordeaux, in south west France, and placed in a detention camp. Admiral Scheer eventually reached Kiev on April Fool's Day, 1941, sinking sixteen ships in all, before meeting the same fate in the same month four years later.

(By the by – and you'll be desperate to hear it – Admiral Scheer had wreaked absolute havoc on the working class districts of the undefended southern Spanish port of Almería one fine day in May, 1937, as a reprisal for the Spanish Republic's bombing of the cruiser Deutschland two days earlier. They didn't wait around, those Huns.)

That much is true and verifiable. What happened to Sammy and his mates thereafter is a mixture of truth, conjecture and legend.

Having now acquired, at the age of eighteen, the features of a man of fifty, and a Liverpool accent which at times defied comprehension, "Me an' a few of the lads, like, decided to escape". They made their uncertain way southwards with the intention of somehow crossing into Spain, neutral in World War Two, having just finished its own appalling Civil War (though Franco was still having a ball by executing as many former enemies as he could find).

The tale is that in a French/Spanish border bar, Sammy and chums got blind drunk, and raucously sang patriotic songs which included scurrilous remarks about the German people in general, and Hitler's private parts in particular.

Needless to say – but I will – they were picked up, roundly thrashed by the Huns, eventually being trucked in open railway wagons somewhere eastwards. Sammy, never forthcoming at the best of times, and not a natural conversationalist, was vague about the ultimate destination, though he did say: "It might of been Poland, or somewhere", which didn't exactly narrow it down.

My Mother told me Sammy was reported 'lost at sea', which, of course, he wasn't, but communications and intelligence collecting then were often less than rudimentary in those confused, confusing times. But Sammy's mother did receive a telegram from the British authorities to that effect.

Some months later – and this is where conjecture and legend meld with truth – she got a letter from a French priest, telling her that he'd witnessed Sammy's arrest and deportation. At no time in the next forty years did Sammy ever feel inclined to clarify matters. His invariable comment, when pressed, was: "I don't remember nowt about it".

What seems to be true is that he was so badly beaten after his capture, undernourished and kept in conditions which had a lasting detrimental effect on his health, that he was finally repatriated by The International Red Cross. His mother received the unexpected news of his release by telegram.

Sammy got off the 80 bus on Banks Road and walked down Window Lane, turned right into Shakespeare Street, through the entry behind what was later Jack Corffe's and Waterworth's and Esther's, and went through the back door into his house, emaciated, with a head bursting with experiences he chose never to tell to anybody. The first thing his mother said when he went into the back kitchen was: "And where've you been, you naughty boy. You might of told me you weren't coming home".

In Otway Street there were streamers from house to facing house, and crowds had gathered, forewarned of Sammy's impending arrival. Reluctantly, he was prevailed upon to appear at the front bedroom window, sheepishly acknowledging the cheers and, perhaps, remembering others who would never return to their families.

And down below, The Davies and The Wilkinsons, Jim and the painfully stuttering Hilda, from across the street; Shebby Porter, flat cap, dark waistcoat over a grey pullover, shiny jacket you could see yourself in, hobnail boots; Florrie Ellis, a professional bundle of nerves even then, a famed 'jangler', an ever-present at funerals and accidents; Dixons, and Miss Kelly (and her sugar butties); Irish Mrs. Hayes, red eyed, constantly extolling her woes about her wildly imaginative son and her wayward daughter with the very long legs. People from up and down The Lane and the streets that crossed it, all out for a sighting of the reluctant hero, Mr. and Mrs. Burnett's youngest lad, home from The War, and just look at his face, see what them Germans, the bastards, must of done to him, Good-God-Almighty. Shame, it is, a crying shame, poor lad, and him never done no-one no harm, he didn't.

So, Sammy married May Hargreaves, worked irregularly on Garston Docks, spent considerable periods of time on the dole, developed a bad stomach, continued to age prematurely, lived a life with few bright intervals, never complained, never knew what it was to have money, never mind go on holiday. Even we went on holiday. Every year, to Sandymount, Dublin.

"How are you, Sam?"

"Oh, all right, you know, like, Liz."

Years and years of unfulfilled hopes and aspirations, all grown up long before the proper time, no juvenile joys, no young man's flings. Days and weeks endlessly similar, and little light at the end of the tunnel. But Sammy refused to complain. Perhaps he didn't know how to give voice to his thoughts.

Only now can I hope to imagine his daily, weekly, yearly routine of irregular work on Garston Docks, punctuated by long periods when signing on the dole was the central feature of his life. And the almost daily visits to our house at 63 Otway Street, no great thrill in anybody's life, I have to tell you.

Once in a while, when he was working and a banana boat docked, he'd come to our house at night and hand my Mother a great bundle covered in an old sheet or a threadbare piece of clothing. Dozens of bananas for the cupboard under the stairs, almost emerald green and as hard as truncheons, awaiting their time to ripen in the warmth and the darkness.

One Christmas, back in the fifties, which looked as though it was going to be indistinguishable from any other day of the year, and another bundle from Sammy. His face was red-raw from the biting wind, his eyes streaming. It was a turkey from the back yard of a house at the bottom of Shakespeare Street, and its neck hung limp and listless. Sammy and George had lain in wait for weeks and weeks, bided their time, struck decisively, and numbers 45 and 63 and 69 Otway Street, Garston, Liverpool 19 had a memorable Christmas.

One day – I can't remember when, nor the circumstances, since Sammy's visits merged one into another, seldom different – one day, he seemed to have been standing in his usual position for ages. My Mother busied herself around the house, as usual, and Eileen was in and out, looking for something she might borrow, to forestall the need to go out and buy it: she resented having to change a ten-bob note. "Have you got a cup of sugar, Liz?" or "Would you have enough for Our Sheel's dinner, Liz?" Anyway, eventually Sammy went with "See you again, Liz", and for some reason I ran after him.

Out into the back yard, up the back entry to the top, turned right, across the top of Otway Street, and saw Sammy's hunched form receding in the poor light. Called his name and blubbered something, pressed a half crown into his hand. Ran back home in the growing gloom and cried and cried and cried, speechless and angry, without knowing why. Fifty odd years later and it still troubles me, but at least I now know why I cried.

So, there you have it, a basically authentic little tale of little people with big hearts. Garston Under The Bridge was full of such people, their lives lived in almost total anonymity, whose little triumphs and frequent falls deserve a voice.

Tommy Hughes and Paddy Larkin, John and Mary, Hilda and Les Jones, Ronnie Evans, Ruth Glennon, Carol Brown and an endless litany of others. So many, many people who left their mark somewhere and somehow in ways they'll never know. But we'll know, won't we. Somebody's got to tell these stories of people whose worth is far, far greater than their achievements, haven't they.

Rhetorical questions. No punctuation marks needed. Don't bother to answer.

10. Stanley Whelan's bells

Canon Henry Moffat, parish priest of Holy Trinity Roman Catholic Church, Banks Road, Garston, Liverpool 19, was a small man, little more than five feet in height. He had snow white pomaded hair, beautifully parted at the side and immaculately barbered, wore black framed spectacles and an elegant black raincoat almost to his ankles, had a fleshy chin, and took no prisoners.

His sermons invariably instructed us what we shouldn't be doing with our lives – the fundamental notions solidly and rigidly based on The Ten Commandments to the exclusion of almost everything else – but I don't have any great memory of his ever speaking at length about the love of God, much the same as most priests of those times.

He and his successors in Holy Trinity – Fathers Lydiate, Leahy, Lynch, Gavin and Monsignor Taylor – coloured and shaped my life for many years after. That's not a complaint, by the way: it's simply the way things were in those days, and a higher ecclesiastic authority than the Canon and his successors should answer for that. The only exceptions I can recall were a lovely man called Father Whyche, and Father Conor Ward.

Father Whyche's almost total blindness never prevented him from decorating his mother's house every year or so. His sermons were all over the place, thematically speaking, but they were honest and human and somehow touched the right spot, and in his short time in Garston he was greatly loved. Father Conor Ward was, quite simply, an enormously gentle, immensely likeable human being, quiet of voice and measured in everything he did and said, with a stunning smile and an Irish accent like honey. He also had university degrees (plural) at the very highest level.

Canon Moffat spoke well. His voice was strong and certain and he was never one to disguise his strongly held opinions. A priest needed to be strong and his flock wanted him to be strong. I recall quite clearly one Sunday morning at High Mass – everything but the sermon, and some of the hymns, in Latin – Veronica getting the benefit of the Canon's forthright opinions.

For years without number, she had, singlehandedly, been the choir (eventually being awarded the Bene Merenti Medal), ready for every call from the Canon, every Novena and Benediction and High Mass, and anything else he chose to organise.

No doubt about it, Veronica was starting to hit a few bum notes – she must have been seventy plus if she was a day, as my Mother would say – that sometimes made you close your eyes and purse your lips and bow your head, but she was loyal beyond the call of duty. So she was understandably miffed when the Canon, from the altar steps as he paraded from the

Sacristy, turned slowly, waited in feigned patience for the end of the entrance hymn, and loudly asked Veronica if she couldn't do any better than that.

"If you think you can do any better, Father", came the clear, measured retort, "you're more than welcome to come up and show us all."

Alongside her, seated at the organ, Miss Merrigan, another old stalwart of countless years, squirmed and waited for the anticipated fall-out.

The Mass started thirty seconds later without further comment on either side (much to Miss Merrigan's relief), and Veronica's musical probity was never again called into question. If the truth be known, deep down – so far down that it was seldom visible – the Canon was very fond of Veronica, and grateful: it's just that he had problems expressing his gratitude. He, too, was over seventy at the time and he'd started at Upholland at the tender age of ten, and his tuition had obviously been lacking in social skills.

Every Friday evening, whatever the weather, the Canon would go out collecting for The Altar Society (which paid for the flowers, candles and other day to day necessities of the Church of Holy Trinity). At least two, and frequently more, of the older altar servers would accompany him on his rounds, knocking on the next few doors in anticipation of the Canon's arrival.

(There was Stephen Hutton, who went to study for the priesthood, impelled by Irish parental enthusiasm and tradition, only to give it up in his late teens; Henry, his younger brother, who was possessed of a wince-making body odour, though he seemed blithely unaware of it; Gerard Raughter, a lovely looking lad from Saunby Street with a strained voice, who died mysteriously in his first year at Liverpool University, one year ahead of me at De La Salle Grammar School, a good footballer and Head Boy of Howard House, if I'm not mistaken; Michael and Frankie Loftus, from Shakespeare Street; Rusty McLoughlin from Saunby Street, and just opposite the Raughters.)

God knows how many insults from lukewarm parishioners, lapsed Catholics, and non-Catholics the Canon had to put up with! Invariably unsmiling and distant by nature and conditioning, he'd pocket whatever Raglan, Byron, Shakespeare and Otway Streets' parishioners could afford, reminding them that he'd be back next month, thanking them by means of a brisk nod of the head.

The Priests' House was a fine building, attached to the church, on the other side of The Cinder Path and looking across The Matchworks' fields. In those days, there were, of course, at least two housekeepers, always Irish and single, less than glamorous, shall we say, but wholesome and red faced with big hands and wide shoulders, who guarded the Canon and his curates with a ferocious, quasi maternal devotion. Few were the parishioners who knocked on the presbytery door and came away verbally unscathed. Additionally, they were all chastely in love with young Jeremiah O'Sullivan, the Canon's strikingly handsome curate from the very bogs of the very bogs of Dear Old Ireland.

Now, to get from the house to the Sacristy, where they vested for Mass or Benediction or Confessions or Novenas, the priests would simply use the internal corridor linking both the church and the Priests' House. So, if you were sampling the sweet altar wine, unseen behind the inner Sacristy door, you at least had the considerable advantage of being forewarned of the priest's approach by his echoing footsteps.

Once, though the Canon didn't actually catch Billy Thornber in the act, Billy foolishly decided to back-chat the Canon, who belted him round the Sacristy with his breviary before starting Mass. Whatever the merits or otherwise of the Canon's aggressive riposte, Billy deserved anything and everything he got: by common consent, he really was a mouthy, cocky little shit of the first order.

The Canon invariably let Richard Ashcroft or one of the other older altar servers – Rusty McLoughlin or one of the Loftus boys – arrange the duties for the following week. At home, I had been instructed to volunteer for Mass every day, and for two Masses on Sunday. My Father had bought me my own black cassock, which I'd bring home to be ironed at the end of High Mass on Sunday. I didn't need it for Sunday School, of course: we just sat there and listened, without understanding a word.

(Oh, and at all costs, you avoided like the very Plague itself going to Confession if the Canon was in session.

"You did what? Oh, my Good God in Heaven! How many times? You didn't, surely!"

And he'd go on in that fashion at the top of his voice. The confessional's closed door afforded not the slightest privacy when Canon Moffat was in full flow, which was every time he was in his confessional.)

High Mass at eleven o'clock on Sunday morning was the high point of the week, and the Canon always officiated. The church building itself lacked even the most minimal quality in terms of ecclesiastical architecture, being simply one nave, with aisles left and right and down the centre; the Lady Chapel half way up on the right hand side, just before the terrifying confessionals (not even remotely terrifying when the wonderfully gentle Father Conor Ward was on duty: "Ah, well now, Jesus will forgive you, my child. Have no doubt about that.").

Behind the High Altar, there were two tall stained-glass windows, the only ones in the entire church, one of Saint Henry, the other of Saint Jeremiah. They looked enormously impressive when the sun shone through them in the earlier part of the day, and they especially looked a treat at High Mass on Sunday.

At the very back of the church, just beneath the choir loft, the collectors placed themselves importantly, ready to burst into action, all four of them, with the collection plates either side of Communion: Dick Ashcroft, Tommy Hughes, Frankie Loftus's dad and Joe Whelan. For some reason, my Father used to call them The Gestapo. And another mystery for me: before he went to receive Communion, he'd take out his false teeth and put them in his pocket. My Father, not the Canon, you understand.

Anyway, back to High Mass, Sunday morning at eleven o'clock sharp, and make sure you're on time, too.

Invariably, there'd be at least ten altar servers: two acolytes, one on the thurible (or the thurifer, as my Father called it), Richard Ashcroft as Master of Ceremonies (and a priesthood that never lasted more than a few years). They, and the Canon, would be on the High Altar itself, the Mass in Latin, the Canon with his back to the congregation. In the Sanctuary, three on either side, would be six other altar boys, younger and deemed not worthy yet of the High Altar, each one with a candle. Followed by Canon Moffat.

And may God help you, as the Canon passed, if he saw anything untoward about your stance or the fall of your cotter. There would be a resounding crack as the Canon's breviary came into brief but painful contact with the back of the head of the altar boy judged to have erred. Worse would follow if your candle shed wax on the mustard coloured carpet of the Sanctuary. Stanley Whelan had a noticeable – and what seemed like a permanent – lump on the back of his head.

Then, the mystery of the Mass would begin – a mystery, since nobody could understand the Latin and the altar boys' responses. Later, the sermon, with its menace of Hell and all its pains and torments, and for all eternity, the Canon frequently stopping to berate late comers with "Do come right up to the front. No, no. Up here. Plenty of room at the front, though The Lord Himself knows why anybody could possibly be late for the eleven o'clock Sunday Mass". And the late comers, mortified and embarrassed, sweating prodigiously, head down and silent under the measured rebukes, did their best to disappear into an imaginary hole deep in the ground.

At five minutes to eleven on that memorable day, I was the only altar boy kitted out for High Mass. I'd never been in a situation of such terrifying responsibility before, and Canon Moffat was clearly a worried parish priest, casting dubious glances in my direction, very clearly unsure of my suitability in the circumstances.

The Big Six were lit – and it took me ages and ages, reaching and sweating to light them, hot candle wax dripping on my heavily perspiring forehead, me cursing colourfully even at that age and in such hallowed surroundings. The water was all ready for the Aspergus Me, wine and water cruets correctly in place on the little green marble ledge to the right of the High Altar, the altar gates open and ready for the Canon's entrance. And a ten year old altar boy sat in the Sacristy, almost physically sick with fear and the possibility of failure, followed by terrifying retribution.

At one minute to eleven o'clock, Stanley Whelan crashed through the Sacristy's double doors, dishevelled hair in every direction, nose running and sweat coursing down his face, jacket flying rebelliously behind him, and informed me that "Am on them bells today, O'Neill!".

Let's pause for a minute, if you will.

The Canon, not what you might call an ecclesiastical innovator, had, for reasons still unexplained to this day, decided to buy a new set of hand bells from The Catholic Truth Society, to be rung at significant parts of the Mass: to wit, the Sanctus, and the Consecration. He'd gone further and purchased a gong, which would be struck solely at the Elevation of The

Host and the Elevation of The Precious Blood. And that particular Sunday was to witness its debut.

Somehow, Stanley, who wasn't down to serve High Mass that week, as it turns out, had found out that those on the servers' list for High Mass wouldn't be there: Father O'Sullivan, forgetting to tell the Canon, was taking the annual altar boys' outing to Blackpool on that very day.

My Father had previously excused me from going – what, enjoying yourself on Sunday, even if Jeremiah O'Sullivan tacitly disagreed! – hence my presence at church that day. Stanley was there because – surprise, surprise! – he'd only remembered about the altar boys' outing when he saw the bus disappear down Banks Road in the direction of Saint Mary's Road and beyond, so he thought he'd take advantage of their absence.

So, one altar boy, in meticulously ironed cassock and Persil-white cotter, and another, who looked as if, just that minute, he'd been in a fight with militant members of the Orange Lodge Parade in Window Lane, walked ahead of Canon Henry Moffat, through the open altar gates and onto High Altar, Stanley hefting the thurible as if it were a caber.

The Aspergus Me went moderately well, except that Stanley dropped an over-flowing water boat half way down the aisle, and got cuffed by the Canon, and rightly so, in full view of all the faithful of Holy Trinity Roman Catholic Church, Garston, Liverpool 19.

The bells, administered in an anarchic manner by a now clearly deranged Stanley, were rung at approximately the correct moments, encouraged by the Canon's withering looks, but the gong was something else, as they say.

There was a stick with a head of leather-covered wood attached to the shaft, and the requirement was – at the Elevation of The Bread, and, some very short time later, of The Precious Blood – to smite the gong clearly and cleanly with the leather-covered head of the stick.

Stanley, by now manic, a strange look in his eyes beneath his wet, flopping, sweating fringe, managed with all his might and a distinct shortage of science to twat the wooden stick, instead of the leather-covered head, three times against the gong, making the most hideous noise. The Canon, as you might expect, was enraged, but managed to content himself (if such is the best word to use) with another withering look in Stanley's direction, which would have destroyed any normal mortal. But Stanley was unmoved, oblivious to everything, clearly out of the game, as they say, and quite obviously in a world of his own making.

At the Elevation of the Precious Blood, he brought the stick down on the gong from such a height that it splintered and flew off in a hundred directions, the disconnected leather-head of the stick just missing one of the Big Six.

Surprising though it may seem, I can't remember what immediately followed, except that there was a scream of naked pain from the direction where Stanley was performing, part of the shaft still firmly grasped in his sweaty hand. The rest is just a blur and open to interpretation.

Suffice it to say that Stanley was summarily expelled from the altar, followed by language you don't normally associate with a Canon of The Roman Catholic Church; though the meaning and symbolic importance of the expulsion were totally lost on Stanley, who promptly forgot the whole disaster with the most consummate ease, and turned up the following Sunday as if nothing untoward had happened.

Oh, and as something of a post script, I have to tell you – though you may suspend belief after reading much of the above – that Canon Henry Moffat was hugely respected (and sometimes loved) by most of his parishioners.

Honest to God!

People were like that then.

11. I remember the day …

I remember the day and the time that Frankie Jones died. It was half an hour after midnight on 24th. August, 1976. I remember it so well.

I'd just finished the midnight 'milk run', a phrase we laughingly conjured up to represent the gut-churning nappy changing and bottle feeding in the hours when we should have been asleep. 'Midnight' was any time in the hours of darkness, for us.

Subdued activity, rather than the instant crying we'd experienced with our first born's every waking hour, gave warning that Number Two was on the move.

There was no mistaking the smell when I went in. The baby had crawled to the side of the cot, somehow dragged herself upright, and stood there in discoloured baby-grow, an enormous bulge between her legs, a radiant smile on her face in the relief of yet another job well done.

I picked her up gingerly, gave her something of a distant hug, put her on her back on the changing mat, set to work against a background of infantile noises of gratitude and pleasure. I put the foul smelling nappy in a bucket in the bathroom.

By the time I got back, the clever little thing had done another load. Holding my breath and checking a movement in the lower reaches of my stomach, I did the needful, pinned on a nappy like an ill fitting turban, picked her up, and briefly carried her over to the window to see if anybody else was foolish enough to be up at that hour.

I looked at Mickey Mouse, who indicated that it was twenty minutes to one o'clock, but it would be quite a few minutes yet before Number Two would be ready to go down. She'd firmly thrust her bottle to the corner of her mouth, resolutely refusing to drink the muck, a smile on her face – or wind – to celebrate her little victory.

Slowly we edged towards the cot. To my surprise, she made no protest when I laid her down. Rodney Dwarf was already comfortably installed, and within minutes his little human friend had unexpectedly joined him in the Land of Nod.

I was wide awake now. Deciding against going back to bed straight away, I eased down the stairs with exaggerated care.

That's when the phone trilled.

"Good-Jesus-Tonight!"

My Mother and most of the other female members of my family had always greeted the arrival of a letter or some unexpected piece of news in much the same way. So, for the phone to ring at such a time, the more so when I was totally unprepared for it, well, what could you expect me to say!

"You can guess what it is, can't you?"

"What?"

"You can guess what it is." There was a pause. "It's Frankie Jones."

"What is?"

"It's Frank. He's gone."

"Gone where?"

"It's Frank." It was my brother's voice. "He's dead."

Margaret was at the top of the stairs by now, her hair pointing in all directions, lines and creases on her face where she'd briefly lain on the pillow. I failed to give a reply to her question which had not yet registered.

"What's the matter?" More insistent this time, more demanding of an answer.

"It's Frank. Frankie Jones. He's dead."

"Oh, my God! When?"

"This morning ... About midnight, he says ... Or sometime ... In Sefton General, he says ... I didn't even know he was bloody well ill ..."

Pause.

"Coffee?"

"What?"

"Coffee. Will I make you a cup of coffee?"

"I've got to go. I've got to go and see Eileen."

"What can you do, though? There's nothing you can do"

"I've still got to go:"

"I'll get you a coffee. Just sit there. Won't be a minute."

I heard her muted movements in the kitchen, but they failed to register, had no significance for me. The children in bed and Frankie Jones dead! My Uncle Frankie Jones, not yet fifty! Good-Jesus-Tonight!

We never again spoke about those moments in the early hours of that August summer morning, that monumentally hot summer when it failed to rain for eight long weeks and more, the inflatable pool in the middle of what was once called a lawn of sorts in Holmville Road, Higher Bebington, until the sun baked it a golden yellow, and me, unshaven for all eight weeks, generous summer holidays from Liverpool College.

"Will you be all right?"

"Yes. Yes, I think so."

"Phone?"

"What?"

"Phone me. Give me a call?"

"I will, yes. Later in the morning, though, eh?"

I backed out the Volkswagen, waved mechanically, and went to see Frankie Jones' new widow.

It had been years since I'd driven through the Mersey Tunnel. Not surprisingly, at that hour, there was very little traffic about.

Lights in the Tunnel's roof flashed uniformly above me. A long straight, now winding expansively round a bend or two, two cars passing me in the opposite direction. At the other end, momentarily confused by the new one way system, I was thankful I was able to navigate it without the discomfort of hooting horns and mouthed invective in some frenetic morning or evening rush hour.

Sand blasted Law Courts on the right, standing out proudly against the less than totally dark sky. Further on, the naked ugly giant of the statue above and astride Lewis's front door (which you could just about see from Derek Lomax's classroom at the top of the Victoria Building at the top of Mount Pleasant). And it needed a conscious effort on my part to bring my mind back to the reason for being in the middle of a deserted and not totally unattractive city at twenty minutes to two on an August morning in 1976.

If I saw or recognised successive sights and landmarks remembered from The Wonderful Sixties, they made no impression on me. Around each bend and along each straight I saw Frankie Jones' face, with background details, a face I hadn't seen for a few years.

(Somewhere I know I have a photo of him. I must try and find it, though I don't need it, because even now I can recall its every detail. High forehead below whispy black, tangled hair, lively eyes always ready for unconventional, unorthodox humour, invariably at his own expense, large, aquiline nose and prominent chin, lovely man.)

We'd gone down one Christmas and seen him for the first time since our wedding four years previously. Yet his instantly bright welcome was as if no time, no incidents, had intervened. Not an effusive welcome, but a simple acceptance of our unexpected visit, without the need to explain or apologise for long absences, the understanding that people had new features of their lives to come to terms with, new duties to perform and new allegiances to satisfy.

(I remember we'd sit together and watch 'The Untouchables', Elliot Ness and Frank Nitty in black and white. It was strange: Frank was, in every sense, the mildest man you could come across, but he had a passion for knowledge about Hitler and Stalin and Al Capone, for 'True Crime' and his detective magazines and his boxing monthlies and weeklies – he had a knee-high pile of 'The Ring' at the side of his armchair that he got from the newsagent that sold dirty books at the bottom of Saint Mary's Road, just opposite the church yard where Frankie Jones would lie forever a week after that August morning.

Other than The Echo and The News of The World and Reveille, he never read anything else. So it was something of a surprise when he asked me to lend him 'In Cold Blood', which he read cover to cover in one sitting, enthralled.)

On my left, at the top of Dock Road, The Lyceum, scene of a prodigious lie that I scandalously got away with, all boarded up. Unrecognisable, now, as the by-pass swings wide and smooth around Garston, so that you won't see The Mona or The Bridge or Billy the Bookie's. The road dips at the bottom of The Village and I stop at the lights outside Ellis the Newsagent.

(I remember going to school with him, Ellis' lad – well, not exactly with him, but I remember he was in the Sixth Form at De La Salle Grammar School when I first started: a blue jowelled youth of sixteen or seventeen, with a short-back-and-sides, white socks, winkle pickers, an attitude, as they say. Face like a smacked arse, as Peggy would say.)

Since I first knew Frank, twenty-some years ago as a small child, I'd never addressed him in any other way than by his Christian name, even though he was my uncle and an adult. There seemed to be no need for titles, no need to stand on any ceremony, because with him it was totally out of place. And as an older child, a teenager, I'd often go in just to sit in his company, few words spoken because there seemed no necessity.

"Homework, son?"

"Yes, Frank. I've got stacks of it tonight."

"And how you getting on at your new school, then, all right?"

"Great, really. But I can't do me algebra."

"I was never any good at languages, neither."

Then, he'd return to The Echo, bicycle clips still around his working jeans, the cat comfortably on his knee, his evening meal tray at his feet and a fire blazing up the chimney.

Even when I left school and changed my allegiances and superficially became sophisticated and more than mildly obnoxious, I'd still go in and sit with Frank. Sometimes, I'd have to climb over the back yard wall because he hadn't heard my knock on the front door.

"Hey! It's a bloody good job you came in and woke me up when you did! You know what I'm like. If I fall asleep for just five minutes before I go to bed, that's it. I'll be awake all night long, I will."

"I thought so, Frank. That's why I climbed over the wall."

"Good job you did, son. Eileen's gone the bingo again. Won't be back until about ten. Gone with Peggy, I think. Want a cup of tea or something?"

"I'll put one on, Frank. Two sugars?")

I turned right under The Bridge, swinging left beneath the church yard, past The Gas Works, right turn down The Lane, looking like Beirut.

The whole place seemed claustrophobic to me – the houses and shops, puny and shabby; new, ugly maisonettes where the Co-Op used to be, with its pulleys which took your change from counter to till and back again; Jimmy Lunt's, all boarded up now, smells and sights locked up forever; and Esther's, just across the road, pyramids of wool symmetrically sited in the display window; Humes', and the memories of meat pies and coffee buns; Jack Corffe's, who worked every hour he could to put his two lads through Liverpool College at a time when 'private education' was not a widely understood concept.

There were two cars already outside the house, number sixty nine, both of which I recognised. I still hadn't really grasped the significance of my own presence at two fifteen in the morning at the little terraced house in the street where I'd spent my first twenty years, at number sixty three.

If it hadn't been for the street light high above Shebby Porter's front door on the opposite side of the street, the bedroom would have been in complete darkness. The curtains were uniformly drawn aside and the lower window pane had been raised a few inches in an effort to make the warm night more comfortable. The same window where Sammy waved to the crowds down below when he came back from The War, its indelible mark on him throughout his sad life.

I stood there for a few minutes, convinced I'd entered the wrong bedroom of the two. There was no sound, no movement, simply a tangible presence, and when I turned away from the window the bulk on the opposite wall registered.

"Oh-Good-Jesus-Tonight, Eileen!"

She was sitting on the bed, full length, her back against the head board, fully dressed, coat still buttoned, scarf still on her head. Later, I learned she'd gone directly to the bedroom from the hospital, an hour before my arrival.

"That you, Eileen?"

An inane question, but I couldn't find anything else to say. There was no answer, and I moved to the side of the bed and gently sat on the edge. After what must have been minutes, I spoke.

"What can I say, Eileen?"

All the way over, in the car, I'd practiced my part, visualised the scene, the people with their hushed and respectful voices, the red rimmed eyes and the nose blowing and the smell of stewed tea and the gentle closing of doors, and this was all I could manage to say. She made no answer and I dried up.

I put an arm uncomfortably, self consciously around her, and gradually the stiffness left her body and she leaned against me, no sound yet, no verbal reaction. Then the sensation of tears silently shed, a more noticeable movement of her body, still no sound, as she shook more, and then her whole body given over completely to my support as repressed emotions welled up again.

I'd known Eileen longer than Frank. She was no more than fifteen years older than I was. When my own Mother threw me out into the back entry after yet another emotional crisis, school books and school bag following me through the air, it was Eileen who'd taken me in and let me do my homework in the back kitchen on the work surface Frankie Jones had made alongside the cooker.

"What's up with her now, love? Your Mum, what's up with her now, then?"

"Don't know, Eil."

"Never mind, then. You just sit there and I'll make you a nice cup of tea. You never mind."

And again, the unspoken belief, lore in my family, in the curative powers of a nice cup of tea and a good sit down.

It had been Eileen, too, who'd been instrumental in getting permission for me to go to Garston Baths with the school. ("For God's sake, Lizzie, he's not gonna drown!")

"And I'm only forty!"

"What's that, Eil?"

"I'm only forty. I might be another forty years like this. What am I going to do?"

It was as if I weren't there. She was merely thinking aloud.

"I mean to say, how can I go out into the street, and people knowing what's happened? I could be like this for another forty years. What am I going to do? I'm only forty now, you know. I mean to say, what am I going to do now?"

There was no answer to that, neither then nor afterwards. Nor for many years afterwards.

"He just said he had a head ache, that's all. And then he sat down on the yard floor, over by the back door ... Just a head ache, that's all he said it was ... By the time we got to the hospital ... But they wouldn't even let me go in the ambulance ... Nor Peggy, they wouldn't let her go, neither ... By the time we got there he was gone ..."

Pause.

"They wouldn't let me and Peggy see him. One of them nurses just came over and said she was very sorry indeed to have to tell us but he was gone, just before we got there."

Pause.

"What am I going to do now?"

Again I made no answer, hoping that my tighter grip around her body would somehow be sufficient to let her know that we'd all try to help her through it.

"How's the kids, love? And Margaret?"

What is it, I thought, then and many times later, that makes people in sudden grief and abject misery ask about others and their puny, day to day existences, inconsequential, given the circumstances. It was almost as if she wanted to distance herself from the stigma of her loss, as if something dirty and shameful and disfiguring had happened to her; almost as if she felt some guilt and needed to change the subject, alter the focus, draw a veil over things.

In subsequent years and similar circumstances of bereavement, it was something I reluctantly got used to, though I continue to marvel at it.

"They're fine. One of them's got a cold, but, you know ..."

Maybe I was helping her, I thought later, but I was ashamed of myself, discussing something that had not the slightest relevance to the awful present.

"Have you had a cup of tea?"

"What's that, Eil?"

"Cup of tea. Peggy'll get you one if ..."

"It's all right, Eil. I'll get one after. I'm all right, thanks."

And I remembered Eileen's cups of tea, always too weak and too milky and seldom better than lukewarm. And the baked beans she cooked me because my own Mother didn't like 'smells like that' in her kitchen. And her sprouts, like soup.

The cold nights with the logs on the fire, horded from The Matchworks, the cat on my lap and my legs burning, and the lukewarm tea and the butter-dripping toast passed over the back of the sofa. The Test Card on the television and Roger Bannister staggering through the tape again in black and white; and Griffin scoring for West Brom in the last minutes of the Cup Final. Jim Reeves, dead in a plane crash in far away Idaho, forty years old: "Adiós, amigo, Adiós, my friend".

What had happened to all those years, all so full of different emotions? The smells and the colours and the sounds?

Where did all the people go?

What happened to 'her from down the back entry' whose red headed son bore not the slightest resemblance to painfully meek Vic? And Shebby, who lived in the bare house across the road with his son and his nephew? And Kelleher, with his beak of a nose, who told me about 'this group' long before they found lasting fame as The Beatles? Bert Savage, and Melvin and Robin Corrie from next door? Norman and Sylvia and Florrie Ellis? All gone as if they never existed outside of the imagination.

"And he was no trouble at all. No trouble at all, he wasn't. He'd come home, and if his tea wasn't ready, he'd just go up to the allotment, or his pigeons ..."

"D'you remember that day he came back ..."

"... and someone had got in and killed them all? I do, that. As if it was only yesterday. D'you know, he never kept pigeons after that. Never found out who it was, neither."

I looked around the room where Frankie Jones had slept and where he had sired just once in his twenty two years of married life.

"Your Mother's downstairs. And Anthony came as soon as they knew. He ran your Mum down here."

"Yes, I know, Eil."

It was ineffectual, redundant and inconsequential, but I was at a loss to say anything meaningful or profound. What can you say to a woman of forty whose husband's been lost to her in the blinking of an eye, there one moment and inexplicably gone the next?

I slept on the sofa in number sixty three – Peggy and George had moved from forty five, on the end of the block. Slept and honked like a goose until I fell asleep.

Late that afternoon, we went up to the funeral home in Heald Street with Eileen to see Frank laid out in the same light green suit he'd been married in twenty-odd years before. When I was eventually persuaded to look at him, I brushed his forehead, cold as marble, with my mouth, and I fled in pain and anger with a bottomless hole in my chest, hurting and sobbing like a child, such was the intense feeling of loss.

Three days later, cars at sixty nine, Otway Street. Sammy with Roy and May and Lyn; Georgie and Peggy and Our Dennis and Lesley; my Mother and Father and brother; Uncle Frank and Auntie Winnie from Childwall, just off the 66 bus in Window Lane. All looking at each other, shaking their heads, words superfluous, eyes expressing everything needed.

Wilks and Puddin English and his brother, and the Davies's, Dixons, all at their front doors across the street. Eyes downcast and sorrowful and respectful in their silent witness. Good people quietly mourning a wonderful, truly wonderful man.

Up the top of the street, barely twenty yards, and left into Window Lane at a snail's pace to the junction at the top. People lining both sides, no moving traffic. No buses passing.

Right at the Gasworks and slowly past Banks Road School and Top Park on the right, Holy Trinity on the left. Then a long, left loop past the old aerodrome on the right, Bryant & May's fields on the left (where, still not yet in his teens, Our Dennis put the very fear of God into a forty-something who called us 'Catholic bastards').

Left into Speke Road, where Eileen was to live alone and bitter and jealous and uneven-tempered and in increasingly poor health in a tiny flat for another twenty, largely unhappy, years.

Pavements on both sides of the wide Speke Boulevard and the grassed medium packed two and three deep with silent, head bowed people. Women with head scarves, men in overalls, all from The Matchworks, the machines stopped in tribute and respect for a colleague whose only words of anger were: "Oh, for God's sake, Eileen, just drop it!"

I don't remember much more. I don't want to remember any more. It still hurts. Forty plus years later, and it still hurts, very badly.

12. Hindsight

From as far back as I can recall of my first dozen or so years at 63, Otway Street, Garston, Liverpool 19, I hated Sundays. It was supposed to be a day of rest, a day you did things you couldn't do during the timetabled week days, a change from the normal routine. But Sunday tended to impose a timetable of its own, and more often than not it was less than happy. Sorry to be so direct at this early stage in the narrative: you wouldn't want us to get off on the wrong foot with euphemistic remarks you could see through, would you, Reader?

I suppose it was natural – or maybe it was the very opposite: unnatural – that in our semi Catholic Garston household Sundays meant going to church. Lots and lots of going to church: overkill, you might justifiably say, with later, albeit temporary, consequences.

Sunday effectively started late Saturday afternoon with the dreaded weekly Confession with the redoubtable Canon Henry Moffat. And when he moved on – where on earth did he go, there one day (and for countless years thereafter) and seemingly gone the next, leaving only indistinct memories, the majority of them tinged with regret and a certain lack of happiness – as I say, when he moved on, along came Monsignor Cyril Taylor from an administrative life lived in and around the Curia offices of The Metropolitan Cathedral of Christ The King (or what there was of it at that time). Confessions with The Monsignor were certainly thorough, but without the fear instilled by The Canon. No shouting, no threats, no theatre; just in and out with a whopping penance of prayers: dozens of Our Fathers, Hail Marys and Glory Be to The Fathers, with a Hail, Holy Queen thrown in for good measure. Actually, it did us no harm, if the truth be known, and you felt fairly good after it, all shriven and back on speaking terms with Him, so to speak.

So, Sunday would dawn, and that meant nothing to eat or drink before the eight o'clock Mass, which I always served whether or not I was on the altar boys' rota (which probably negated its authenticity, but that's another story). Home to breakfast and back in the Sacristy of Holy Trinity Church for eleven o'clock, the High Mass, with the Big Six lit and Veronica up in the choir loft, warbling and caterwauling, at least a dozen altar boys at the ready, marshalled by Dick Ashcroft's lad. Invariably, back in the afternoon for Rosary and Benediction with unmarried Josie Donnelly and Tommy Hughes and a few other regulars (with nothing to do on

Sunday afternoons. Then again, maybe they liked Rosary and Benediction – who am I to judge!).

(May – in particular – and October being the months of Our Lady, most of the school turned out for the processions to honour The Mother of God. Down the centre aisle of the church, white shirts and white blouses and veils and a royal blue sash, all organised by the wonderful Miss Coleman, briefly turning left onto Banks Road for a dozen yards or so, left again up the Priests' Path and back into the church via the steps to the Sacristy's side door. Similarly in June, but this time the sash was red for the month of The Sacred Heart.)

After High Mass it was home to lunch and my Mother in the back kitchen with her 'bad stomach' – something of a family legacy, true or imagined: I'm not sure which – whilst we three sat at the table under the stairs. Listening to shouting Billy Cotton with Alan Breeze and Kathie Kay on the wireless, or Radio Eiran, with its jigs and accordion music, which, to these childish ears, all sounded the same, and 'The School Around The Corner' and other attention riveting programmes. (Have you picked up on the sarcasm, Reader?)

Sometimes there'd be a diversion. People shouting excitedly outside in the street, the sound of footsteps running up to the top to the Pye's house on Window Lane, and the Orange Lodge in their berets and pill-box hats and hand bags and bowler hats, banging the very be-jaysus out of their drums, swollen cheeks blowing their instruments, faces like smacked arses, not a smile between them, backs guardsman rigid, Christian sentiment patently absent.

Left to the top of The Lane and turning left down Banks Road, swinging right past Saint Michael's Church and left at the traffic lights and left again up Saint Mary's Road and gone (to wherever they went in their quest for further enjoyment).

Or I'd sneak into Eileen's and read the semi salacious News of The world – 'All human life is there' – and talk to Frank, just home from his precious pigeons for whatever might be on offer for Sunday lunch. There was always a pan of sprouts on the stove, simmering away endlessly, eventually looking like a thick green soup of dubious origin, or, perhaps, like mulched sea weed. In all probability, Frankie Jones liked sprouts, and liked them done that way. Whether he did or not, that's the way he got them. Every Sunday without fail, come rain or shine, as they say.

Or we'd sit on our front step, Dennis and me, and play soldiers or invent stories based on 'Journey into Space'. He was Doc and I was Lemmy, and we'd scare the shit out of each other the way they did on the wireless. Dennis was a past master at scaring the shit out of people: he had a gift that way. The only thing we'd have to look out for was bad tempered Gilly Ireland and his stick, coming up from the bottom end of the block, flat capped head down and swearing to himself about some imagined injustice done to him by the world in general and Garston and Otway Street in particular. Cranky old bastard.

On those seemingly interminable summer Sunday afternoons, the Street Singer would make his slow way up the middle of the street, an elderly man, meticulously dressed in the same suit he must have been demobbed in ('Don't laugh at me 'cos I'm a fool', and 'I'll take you home again, Kathleen' and 'A mother's love's a blessing'). And a door would scratch open in the hot stillness and a turbaned woman would run over and stop him and wordlessly press a coin into his hand and scurry back into her house, banging the door shut behind her.

On he'd go to the top of the street and turn right and make his way down the length of the next street; and I'd sit with tears rolling down my face, trying to hide them from Dennis ("What's the matter, Kid?"), unable to explain the bottomless pit of my anger and sadness.

Some Sundays, my Father would take us, my brother and me, on the sixty six bus as far as Woolton Village with the intention of keeping us occupied and away from occasions of sins that had never entered my mind – at least, not for a while thereafter. Inevitably, we'd go for 'a little visit' to some church or other – Saint Mary's, just off Woolton Village, or Saint Anne's on Allerton Road – and walk around Camp Hill, where there was always a Sunday League game going on.

I remember one time we were watching from behind the goal – with real nets, too! – men shouting and crashing into and off each other and swearing and charging shoulder to shoulder with the goalkeeper: peaked cap on his head, knitted woolly pullover rolled up to his chin, thick socks to his knees and shin pads like Sam Bartram or Bert Williams wore in The Charlie Buchan Football Monthly, diving at opponents' feet and being kicked and stamped on and getting up, giving as good as he got, wellying the lead-heavy ball up field, turning back to his line and inspecting his wounds in a matter of fact manner, dusting off the mud and spitting on his gloves, sharing a remark with a spectator, ready for the next attack, his knees all bloody through the mud.

One of the outfield players thundered a shot at goal, but it was going wide until I put my head down and headed it back into play. The game stopped and everyone looked with open mouths at an eight year old child still standing there, only marginally groggy in spite of the cannonball shot, eyes visibly watering, mouth clamped resolutely shut, ever so slightly dazed. Silence, followed by comments from all over the field: "Rum kid you've got there, pal!" and "Good Jesus wept!" and "Is that kid all right?" and "Bloody hell fire, see if he's all right, will you!"

We crossed Menlove Avenue, walked down the long avenue of trees, me holding his hand, all three of us looking back to see if the sixty six bus was coming. Running down the hill to the bus stop outside the gates of

Clarks Gardens, or we'd walk past the cemetery on the left, Springwood Fields on the right, on past Allerton Station and South Liverpool's football ground on the left, over the brow of the hill (where I had a head-on crash in my blue Volkswagen in July 1967) and Cheshire Lines Station, down past the Sir Alfred Jones Memorial Hospital and The Empire cinema, under The Bridge and home via Banks Road.

Home to fairy cake and the crushing boredom of Sunday evening and 'Sing Something Simple' on the wireless: "We invite you to Sing Something Simple, a collection of your favourite songs, old and new (new?), sung by The Cliff Adams Singers, directed by Cliff Adams and accompanied by Jack Emblow on the accordion". And a young child sighed audibly at the dirge-like songs and wished for something more exciting in his young life.

What it might be, this excitement, he was incapable of specifying, but surely to God, he'd think, there must be better ways of spending a Sunday evening. But occasionally, very occasionally, there'd be an exception to the dirge of dreary Sundays.

My Father had a heavy Raleigh bike, second hand, of course, all oiled and working perfectly, painted black, which he often called his 'life line', to indicate its essential nature in his life, namely, to get him (the four hundred yards or so) to his (irregular) work on Garston Docks.

He was fond of phrases like 'life line' and 'take the bull by the horns' (which he never did, though he encouraged others to do so), 'well, blow me down' (to indicate surprise) and 'that's the limit' (to express frustration), and other highly personalised expressions. And he was utterly unlike his two brothers, Johnny and Michael, my uncles (though I can never remember being aware of any family bond between us. One lived in Derby Street, the other up in the tenements on Speke Road. We saw them, on average, every five years or so, though why escapes me).

The best you could say about Johnny was that he was (fairly) well meaning, cavalier and quixotic, not that he would have understood the last two epithets. By no means did he ever visit hurt on others, but any faint idea of social or family responsibility simply didn't register with him. Michael seemed to amble through life in something of a relatively happy, permanent stupor, with a tacit refusal to admit any sort of complication into his days. He passed on, let's say, in circumstances clouded in mystery. Our Dennis might know. He seems to know everything nobody else knows.

But I digress. Back to my Father's Raleigh.

He'd somehow put together a child's seat behind him, just clearing the back wheel, and a padded leather saddle on the cross bar between his legs. In this fashion, he'd take me and my brother everywhere: up past Dunlop's to Speke Hall; out past The Dam Lane Woods; to Clarks Gardens and Camp Hill; to Saint Anthony of Padua's Church at the bottom of Queen's Drive, the Mossley Hill end (where I ended up as Head of French for four not entirely comfortable years twenty something years later, school six days a week!); to Springwood Fields where, six years or so later, I fell in love with Thomas Hardy's 'The Trumpet Major', encouraged by Bill McHugh at De La Salle Grammar School, God rest him. Read the whole three hundred plus pages under a tree there one hot afternoon, soppy Romantic that I was. I loved Spanish Bécquer and Espronceda, too, and the French Alfreds, de Musset and de Vigny, and Victor Hugo and Lamartine. Oh, happy days! Ha!

Somehow, my Father had contracted an eye infection – from some ship's hold on Garston Docks, one of the banana boats, perhaps – and that whole facial area was hideously swollen. Still on night work, he'd had little sleep for days on end, his head was throbbing, and the whole face was bandaged, leaving him just one red rimmed eye to pilot us safely on the bike. But all three of us, one summer Sunday, played football together on

Springwood for what seemed like hours of headless chicken enjoyment, piles of clothing to represent goalposts, my Father delirious with pain, chasing us and the ball all over the field, shouting and screaming and being children for once.

And it's things like this you remember, isn't it, the good things that lighten the gloom and the darkness, the hindsight that deeply hurts and stings the eyes and constricts the back of the throat and makes you fall silent and pensive, and somehow thankful. So, thank God for People, and thank God for Memories, the good and the not so good. They all have a place, haven't they? Especially the People. Thank God for them.